Cambridge Elements ≡

Elements in Construction Grammar
edited by
Thomas Hoffmann
Catholic University of Eichstätt-Ingolstadt
Alexander Bergs
Osnabrück University

CONSTRUCTIONIST APPROACHES

Past, Present, Future

Tobias Ungerer
Concordia University

Stefan Hartmann
University of Düsseldorf

CAMBRIDGE
UNIVERSITY PRESS

CAMBRIDGE
UNIVERSITY PRESS

Shaftesbury Road, Cambridge CB2 8EA, United Kingdom

One Liberty Plaza, 20th Floor, New York, NY 10006, USA

477 Williamstown Road, Port Melbourne, VIC 3207, Australia

314–321, 3rd Floor, Plot 3, Splendor Forum, Jasola District Centre,
New Delhi – 110025, India

103 Penang Road, #05–06/07, Visioncrest Commercial, Singapore 238467

Cambridge University Press is part of Cambridge University Press & Assessment,
a department of the University of Cambridge.

We share the University's mission to contribute to society through the pursuit of
education, learning and research at the highest international levels of excellence.

www.cambridge.org
Information on this title: www.cambridge.org/9781009308731

DOI: 10.1017/9781009308717

When citing this work, please include a reference to the DOI 10.1017/9781009308717

First published 2023

A catalogue record for this publication is available from the British Library.

ISBN 978-1-009-30873-1 Paperback
ISSN 2753-2674 (online)
ISSN 2753-2666 (print)

Constructionist Approaches

Past, Present, Future

Elements in Construction Grammar

DOI: 10.1017/9781009308717
First published online: June 2023

Tobias Ungerer
Concordia University

Stefan Hartmann
University of Düsseldorf

Author for correspondence: Stefan Hartmann, hartmast@hhu.de

Abstract: Construction Grammar (CxG) has developed into a broad and highly diverse family of approaches that have in common that they see constructions – that is, form–meaning pairs at various levels of abstraction and complexity – as the basic units of language. This Element gives an overview of the origin and the current state of the art of constructionist approaches, focusing, on the one hand, on basic concepts like the notion of "constructions" while, on the other hand, offering an in-depth discussion of current research trends and open questions. The authors discuss the commonalities and differences between the major constructionist approaches as well as the organization of constructional networks and ongoing research on linguistic creativity, multimodality, and individual differences. This title is also available as Open Access on Cambridge Core.

Keywords: construction grammar, cognitive linguistics, usage-based linguistics, network approaches to grammar, linguistic theories

ISBNs: 9781009308731 (PB), 9781009308717 (OC)
ISSNs: 2753-2674 (online), 2753-2666 (print)

Contents

1 Introduction

In this Element, we introduce a family of approaches that regard constructions – that is, form–meaning pairs at various levels of abstraction and complexity – as the main units of linguistic knowledge. Traditional approaches to grammar often assume that our knowledge of language consists of two components: the lexicon as a repository of morphemes, words, and a very limited set of idioms, on the one hand, and the grammar as a set of rules for combining the items in the lexicon on the other (see e.g. Pinker 1994; Taylor 2012). In such approaches, the lexicon is usually kept at a minimum – as Di Sciullo and Williams (1987: 3) famously put it, "[t]he lexicon is like a prison – it contains only the lawless, and the only thing that its inmates have in common is lawlessness." Constructionist approaches take a radically different stance. Their starting point is the observation that there is much more idiomaticity in language than is usually assumed. Broadly speaking, idiomatic units are complex constructions whose meaning cannot be fully derived from their constituent parts (but see Wulff 2008, 2013 for a more nuanced treatment of idiomaticity and its relation to compositionality). Consider, for example, the much discussed *way*-construction, exemplified in (1) (all from the *News on the Web* corpus, Davies 2016–).

(1)   a. Mr. Musk bluffed his way through the crisis. (October 5, 2018, US, *MarketWatch*, NOW corpus)

      b. Last month Tesla CEO Elon Musk bullied his way to reopening his electric car factory in California ahead of local health officials' recommendations. (June 11, 2020, KE, nairobiwire.com, NOW corpus)

      c. Tesla founder and CEO Elon Musk teased his way through the car's introduction, showing pictures of the company's past (April 1, 2016, PK, *BusinessRecorder*, NOW corpus)

      d. Elon Musk tweets his way through his pending Twitter acquisition. (May 21, 2022, US, wral.com, NOW corpus)

As Israel (1996) points out, one important feature of this construction is that it always entails the subject's movement (in a literal or metaphorical sense), even if the lexical semantics of the verb do not imply any kind of movement. Thus, the meanings of the sentences in (1) cannot necessarily be derived from the meanings of their constituent parts. In these examples, the whole is more than the sum of its parts – in other words, we are dealing with structures that are not fully compositional. As we will show in Section 2, the insight that noncompositionality is more ubiquitous in language than one might think was one of the main starting points of constructionist approaches. Language, on this view, is highly idiomatic. Constructionist approaches therefore depart from the classic position that words and morphemes are the main "building blocks" of language that are combined via a set of rules, and instead propose a joint format for the representation of meaning-bearing units of varying sizes and at different levels of abstraction: constructions.

Speaking of "constructionist approaches" underlines that Construction Grammar (CxG), which has grown into a large research field over the last decades with a variety of journals, textbooks, and book series dedicated to it, is not a uniform paradigm but has rather developed into a heterogeneous set of "Construction Grammars," plural (see e.g. Hoffmann 2017a, b). While different approaches differ substantially in some of the assumptions they make as well as in their goals, Goldberg (2013) and Hoffmann (2022: 10–16) summarize four basic assumptions that are common to all "flavors" of Construction Grammar, in addition to the basic concept of linguistic constructions:

- They do not assume a strict division between lexicon and grammar but instead postulate a *lexicon-syntax continuum*.
- They assume that constructions do not exist in isolation and that our knowledge of constructions should not be conceived of as an unstructured list (as is sometimes the case in conceptualizations of the mental lexicon). Instead, they are organized in a taxonomic network, a *construct-i-con*. We will deal with the inner workings of this "grammar network" (Diessel 2019) in Section 4.
- They are *surface oriented*, that is, they do not posit some sort of "deep structure" with abstract syntactic representations and operations. Instead, it is assumed that constructions emerge (historically) and are learned (ontogenetically) via generalizations over concrete instances that language users encounter.
- Given this surface orientation, they do not assume a "Universal Grammar" that underlies all human languages but instead expect a considerable amount of cross-linguistic variability. To the extent that there are universals of language (see Evans & Levinson 2009 for a skeptical stance), they are explained as generalizations deriving from domain-general cognitive processes and functional pressures (Hoffmann 2022: 16).

In the remainder of this text, we will give an overview of the historical development, the current state of the art, and potential future outlooks of constructionist approaches. Of course, many excellent introductions to the framework already exist: for book-length introductions, see Hilpert (2019) and Hoffmann (2022); for chapter-length summaries, see Fried and Östman (2004), Croft and Cruse (2004: 257–290), Croft (2007), Diessel (2015), Hoffmann (2017a) and Boas (2021); see also Hoffmann and Trousdale's (2013) handbook. Compared with these earlier overviews, our focus here will be especially on recent developments in the field, including current research topics as well as ongoing debates that yet need to be resolved.

In Section 2, we provide an overview of the genesis of CxG, before addressing varying definitions of the concept of "construction" and discussing the question of whether morphemes and words should also count as constructions. In Section 3, we compare different constructionist approaches with regard to three parameters: their degree of formalization, their research foci, and the methods they prefer to use. Section 4 focuses on the structure of the construct-i-con, addressing its psychological underpinnings and the different types of links it may contain as well as some open research problems (see also Diessel's [2023] contribution to the *Elements in Construction Grammar* series for an in-depth treatment of constructional networks). Finally, Section 5 discusses some further current developments in CxG, zeroing in on three research topics that have increasingly gained attention in recent years: linguistic creativity, multimodality, and individual differences between language users. Section 6 offers a brief conclusion.

2 Discovering Idiomaticity: The Case for Constructions

2.1 The Early Days of CxG

Historically, the emergence of CxG is closely connected to the endeavor of establishing a counterpart to Chomskyan generative linguistics, which was the dominant paradigm especially in North American linguistics for much of the second half of the twentieth century (see e.g. Harris 2021).[1] While the concept of "constructions" in the constructionist sense as well as the term "Construction Grammar" emerged in the 1980s, especially in the works of Fillmore (1988; Fillmore, Kay, & O'Connor, 1988) and Lakoff (1987), Boas (2021: 43) points out that the intellectual roots of CxG – and of its "sister theory," frame semantics – lie in Fillmore's (1968) seminal paper "The Case for Case." Specifically, he argues that the idea of "deep cases" foreshadows what later came to be known as semantic roles, which in turn play a key role in the interaction of verbs and constructions in CxG. But while the notion of "construction" already appears in earlier works, Fillmore et al.'s (1988) paper on the *let alone* construction is nowadays usually seen as the key starting point of CxG (see e.g. Boas 2021: 49).

Fillmore et al. (1988) argue that idiomaticity is not just an "appendix" to the grammar of the language – instead, idiomatic patterns are themselves productive, highly structured, and worthy of grammatical investigation. In the case of *let alone*, they argue that neither can its properties be exhaustively derived from its lexical makeup and grammatical structure, nor can it be treated as a fixed

---

[1] We can only give a relatively brief overview of the history of constructionist approaches here; for more in-depth discussions, see Boas (2021) and Hoffmann (2017b).

expression. At the syntactic level, Fillmore et al. analyze *let alone* as a coordinating conjunction; at the semantic and pragmatic level, they see it as a paired-focus construction that evokes a certain scale. For example, in (2a), "taking the first step" and "taking the second step" can be interpreted as the contrastively focused elements, and as points on a scale. In (2a), this scale is fairly obvious, as it is in (2b), where *approach* and *equal* can be considered classic examples of lexical items that form a so-called Horn scale, that is, a scale where the stronger term entails the weaker one while the weaker term implicates the falsity of the stronger one (e.g. <*warm, hot*>, <*some, many, most, all*>; see Cummins 2019: 49).

(2)   a. I barely knew what step to take first, let alone what step to take second, let us not talk about the third. (A08, BNC)
       b. The old Herring and Addis tools were made with a finesse and temper that modern tools do not approach, let alone equal. (A0X, BNC)
       c. [R]eference to its existence, let alone study of its function, has been sedulously avoided. (A69, BNC)
       d. I don't have time to feed the children, let alone prepare my lecture. (Fillmore et al. 1988: 531)

In some cases, however, the scales evoked by *let alone* are more complex, as (2c) and especially Fillmore et al.'s example (2d) illustrate: Here, the conjuncts – *reference to its existence* and *study of its function* in (2c), *feed the children* and *prepare my lecture* in (2d) – do not belong to the same semantic domain. Thus, the scales evoked by *let alone* can be strongly context-dependent.

Apart from *let alone*, Fillmore et al. (1988: 510–511) mention a number of other constructions in passing, some of which have been investigated in more detail in later constructionist work; for example, the *what with* construction (*what with the kids and all*; see e.g. Trousdale 2012) and the incredulity response construction (*Him a doctor?!?*; see e.g. Szcześniak & Pachoł 2015). Fillmore et al.'s article thus spawned a series of further constructionist analyses, starting in the early 1990s – for example Kay's (1990) paper on *even* and Michaelis' (1993) study of the English perfect construction – and growing in number ever since.

In the following, we cannot provide a summary of all the phenomena that have been studied from a constructionist perspective over the last thirty-five years, as there are too many. Instead, we will focus on the key notion of "construction," exploring how the concept has developed over time in the context of the changes that CxG as a paradigm has undergone. In particular, we will focus on Goldberg's (1995, 2006, 2019) definitions of constructions, as the evolution of the concept in her writing arguably reflects important developments in CxG, which is why the different definitions she has provided over the years are often cited and compared to each other in introductory texts (e.g. Hilpert 2019; Ziem & Lasch 2013). We will also discuss what kinds of units can be seen as constructions, which naturally depends on the definition of construction that one adopts.

2.2 "Construction": An Evolving Concept

A major contribution to defining the notion of construction was made by Goldberg (1995) in a monograph that also constitutes the first book-length summary of the constructional approach and can therefore be seen as a further milestone in CxG history.[2] In this book, Goldberg outlines many of the key issues that have been at the heart of constructionist approaches ever since: the important role that aspects of meaning (semantic and pragmatic) play in the analysis of grammar; the interaction between constructional meaning and verb meaning; the notion that constructions motivate each other within a network of stored knowledge (see Section 4); and a usage-based account of the partial productivity of constructions based on learning mechanisms such as indirect negative evidence (see Goldberg 2019 for a more recent account of this mechanism in terms of "statistical preemption").

Crucially, Goldberg (1995) also proposes what may be the best-known definition of "construction":

> C is a construction iff$_{def}$ C is a form-meaning pair $<F_i, S_i>$ such that some aspect of F_i or some aspect of S_i is not strictly predictable from C's component parts or from other previously established constructions. (Goldberg 1995: 4)

The definition captures two central elements. First, drawing on the traditional concept of a Saussurean sign (Goldberg 1995: 6), constructions are regarded as units of form that inherently carry meaning, contrary to their generativist conception in terms of meaningless structural rules. In Goldberg's approach as well as subsequent work, "meaning" has come to be understood in a broad sense, comprising lexical, semantic, pragmatic, discourse-functional, and social aspects, while "form" is usually taken to include phonological, syntactic, and morphological information (but see e.g. Herbst & Uhrig 2020 for discussion).[3] Second, Goldberg uses nonpredictability as a criterion for what counts as

---

[2] To be more precise: the first published book-length summary. A CxG textbook by Fillmore and Kay (1993), used in Berkeley linguistics classes, was distributed via a local copy shop (see e.g. www1.icsi.berkeley.edu/~kay/bcg/ConGram.html, last accessed September 14, 2022).

[3] The question of what should count as "form" is where CxG deviates from the related approach of Cognitive Grammar (Langacker 1987): While most Construction Grammarians include syntactic constituents (e.g., NP, VP), syntactic functions (e.g., subject, object), and possibly other grammatical categories (e.g., case, agreement) within the form pole (see e.g. Hoffmann 2022: 39–40),

a construction and what does not: Any pattern that has "unique" properties that go beyond the properties of its subparts and those of other, partially similar, constructions is recognized as a construction in its own right. Nonpredictability is closely linked to the notions of idiomaticity and noncompositionality, which are also often used to argue for the construction status of a pattern (see Pleyer et al. 2022 for the multifaceted meanings of "compositionality"). Crucially, however, the nonpredictability criterion applies not only to idiomatic constructions which, in previous generative work, had been relegated to the "periphery" of language (Chomsky 1981); it also allows for highly frequent and seemingly "regular" or "core" patterns, such as the caused-motion pattern illustrated in (3), to be treated as constructions. The fact that (3b) implies a motion event, even though it contains an intransitive nonmotion verb, suggests that the "caused motion" meaning is associated with the construction itself and is not predictable from the lexical items it contains. As a result, Goldberg's definition allows for a wide view of "constructions" that covers both broad grammatical generalizations and the many less-frequent idiomatic patterns whose role was emphasized by early CxG work.

(3)   a. Pat pushed the piano into the room. (Goldberg 1995: 76)
        b. Sally sneezed the napkin off the table. (Goldberg 1995: 6)

Goldberg's (1995) definition has, however, not remained unchanged over time; rather, it has continued to evolve as subsequent research has brought to light some of its limitations. First, scholars have come to agree that, apart from their nonpredictability, the frequency of linguistic patterns is another major determinant of their status as constructions. Early evidence that speakers track and record frequencies in the linguistic input came from studies showing that more frequent units tend to be phonologically more reduced than less frequent ones (Bybee 2000; Losiewicz 1992). Moreover, the long-standing research on formulaic patterns in language (Bolinger 1976; Kuiper & Haggo 1984; Pawley 1985) has highlighted that speakers rely heavily on lexically fixed chunks in natural speech. As illustrated in (3) and (4), speakers routinely prefer certain frequent expressions over less frequent alternatives, even when the words they contain have similar meanings and they are both sanctioned by the same abstract construction, such as the noun-phrase construction in (4) and the transitive construction in (5). This suggests that speakers store highly frequent chunks as constructions in their own right, even when they can be predicted from their component parts or based on an abstract template they instantiate.

Cognitive Grammar restricts linguistic form to phonological information only and regards "grammatical form" as a reflex of underlying semantic constraints (Langacker 2005: 104–107).

(4)   a. innocent bystanders (preferred)
       b. uninvolved people (dispreferred)

(5)   a. it boggles my mind (preferred)
       b. it giggles my brain (dispreferred)
           (all adapted from Goldberg 2019: 53)

Apart from these fully lexicalized instances, there is also ample evidence that speakers encode frequency information about partially lexicalized subtypes of more abstract constructions. For example, Gries and Stefanowitsch's (2004) corpus results indicate that speakers' use of the ditransitive and the *to*-dative construction varies depending on the verb: While verbs such as *give*, *tell*, and *show* are more often used with the ditransitive, as illustrated in (6), verbs such as *allocate*, *wish*, and *accord* are preferably used with the *to*-dative, as in (7). Even though the sentences in (6) and (7) are all instances of more abstract generalizations, the fact that speakers prefer one variant over the other suggests that they associate distinct frequency-based information with each verb-specific pattern.

(6)   a. She told the children the story. (preferred)
       b. She told the story to the children. (dispreferred)

(7)   a. She allocated the seats to the guests. (preferred)
       b. She allocated the guests the seats. (dispreferred)

As a result, many researchers have argued for the existence of lexically specific constructions even when their form and meaning seem predictable from the more abstract schemas they instantiate (Booij 2002; Bybee & Hopper 2001; Langacker 2005). An often-cited example is *I love you* (Langacker 2005: 140), which, due to its high frequency, is likely to be stored as a separate construction, even though it is fully compositional. Given this evidence, Goldberg (2006) proposed a modified definition of constructions, which explicitly incorporates the frequency criterion and which has again been widely used since:

> Any linguistic pattern is recognized as a construction as long as some aspect of its form or function is not strictly predictable from its component parts or from other constructions recognized to exist. In addition, patterns are stored as constructions even if they are fully predictable as long as they occur with sufficient frequency. (Goldberg 2006: 5)

But the story does not end there, and aspects of the 2006 definition have also come under scrutiny. Zeschel (2009), for instance, raises doubts about the use of the nonpredictability criterion for delineating constructions. In particular, he takes issue with the categorical nature of the criterion: By regarding patterns as either predictable or nonpredictable, analysts are forced to draw sharp distinctions between the features that set apart one construction from another and the ones that fail to do so. As Zeschel (2009: 187–188) argues, however, these decisions are often difficult to make because tests for the presence of a certain feature are not always available; because features might vary in their salience depending on the context; and because interindividual variation among speakers means that constructions are not really characterized by strictly necessary properties but rather by statistical tendencies. Similarly, with respect to compositionality, it has been argued that patterns are not either compositional or noncompositional but that compositionality is a matter of degree (Langacker 2008: 169).

As an alternative to the nonpredictability criterion, Zeschel (2009) advocates the use of Langacker's (1987, 2005) entrenchment criterion, according to which a pattern is recognized as a construction if it is sufficiently entrenched, that is, cognitively routinized (on the concept of entrenchment, see e.g. Blumenthal-Dramé 2012 and Schmid 2017b). Since entrenchment is naturally a gradient concept, this view entails that the distinction between what is a construction and what is not may be continuous rather than categorical, with higher degrees of entrenchment providing increasingly stronger evidence that a pattern has construction status. Crucially, the entrenchment of a unit is commonly assumed to depend on several factors, among them the frequency and the similarity of its instances: The more instances a pattern comprises, and the more similar these instances are to each other (while being simultaneously dissimilar to instances of other patterns), the more likely speakers are to group them together under a construction (Bybee 2013; Schmid 2020; see also Section 4.3 for discussion). Crucially, the notion of similarity is closely related to the nonpredictability criterion used in Goldberg's earlier definitions: The more dissimilar a pattern is to already existing units, the less predictable it is. If, instead, a group of instances are highly similar to an extant construction, they can be subsumed under that generalization, thereby further strengthening it, rather than forming a construction in their own right. The entrenchment criterion, grounded in similarity, can therefore be used to identify constructions in a similar way as the nonpredictability criterion, while simultaneously recasting the distinction in gradient rather than in categorical terms (see later in this section for a discussion of this gradient view).

These comments help explain the differences between Goldberg's earlier accounts and her third and most recent definition of constructions, as stated in her 2019 monograph:

> [C]onstructions are understood to be emergent clusters of lossy memory traces that are aligned within our high- (hyper!) dimensional conceptual space on the basis of shared form, function, and contextual dimensions. (Goldberg 2019: 7)

As is evident from this quote, Goldberg's latest definition completely does away with the notion of nonpredictability. Instead, the similarity among instances is used to group them together in "clusters" that correspond to constructions. Moreover, Goldberg couches her view of constructions in more psychological terms than in earlier definitions, relying on the concepts of "memory traces," "emergent clusters," "conceptual space," and "lossiness." The latter concept is borrowed from computer science and characterizes speakers' memories as partially abstracted ("stripped-down") versions of the original input. The strong psychological component of the definition can be related to theoretical and methodological trends in CxG, where more and more emphasis has been placed on the cognitive reality of constructions, rather than on their description alone, and in which psycho- and neurolinguistic paradigms have become ever more important sources of evidence (see e.g. Hoffmann 2020).

While Goldberg's (2019) definition is the outcome of several decades of constructionist theorizing, it surely will not mark the last attempt to come to terms with the concept of "constructions." One obvious question raised by the definition, for example, is *how much* formal, functional or context- ual information has to be shared by a group of instances (or memory traces) for them to be classified as a construction. Clearly, determining an adequate threshold for similarity is an important task for future empir- ical research (see also Section 4.3). Another striking feature of the 2019 definition is that it no longer makes reference to frequency as a necessary or sufficient criterion for construction status, in contrast to Goldberg's 2006 account (see the earlier definition in this section). This omission is, in fact, intentional, as Goldberg (2019) identifies a problem with the earlier frequency criterion. According to the 2006 definition, a pattern is only recognized as a construction if speakers have witnessed it with sufficient frequency. The paradox that Goldberg (2019: 54) identifies is this: How can speakers accrue experience with a pattern if they only store it once they have already encountered it with sufficient frequency? In other words, if speakers do not retain individual instances of a new pattern, then each newly witnessed instance would seem to be the first of its kind, and speakers would never reach the frequency threshold required for forming a constructional representation. There is, in fact, ample evidence that speakers *do* store single instances of use, also called "exemplars" (Abbot- Smith & Behrens 2006; Ambridge 2020; Bybee 2010). The latter are an important feature of the view of grammar as an emergent system (Hopper 1987) that many cognitive linguists and Construction Grammarians sub- scribe to (e.g. Ellis & Larsen-Freeman 2006; Goldberg 2006; MacWhinney 2019).

Given these arguments, researchers are faced with a potential dilemma: On the one hand, if scholars maintain Goldberg's (2006: 18) well-known claim that "it's constructions all the way down," that is, that speakers' grammatical knowledge *in toto* consists of constructions, then they need to count a single stored exemplar of a new pattern as a construction. This would undermine the frequency criterion of the 2006 definition discussed earlier in this section and allow a potentially exploding number of constructions into the theory. If, on the other hand, scholars reserve the label "construction" for groups of stored exemplars that have grown sufficiently large, then they seem to give up the claim that grammatical knowledge consists of constructions *only*, and instead treat constructions as generalizations over more atomic units.

There are several ways to (potentially) resolve this problem. One rather radical approach would be to abandon the notion of constructions entirely and to reconceptualize linguistic knowledge in terms of a network of associations. Schmid's (2020) entrenchment-and-conventionalization model goes in this direction, although he retains the notion of construction (however, he abandons the idea of constructions as "nodes" in a network; see Schmid 2017a). A second approach would also be quite radical as it would abandon one of the major tenets of CxG: retaining the concept of construction as a heuristic device but dropping the idea that constructions are cognitively plausible entities. This would, however, entail the question of why the concept of constructions is needed in the first place. A third, and potentially the most promising, approach is to adopt a gradualist notion of constructionhood (see Ungerer 2023) – an idea that is also implicit in Goldberg's latest definition and Langacker's entrenchment criterion, as discussed earlier in this section. On this view, construction status is not conceived of as a binary concept according to which a linguistic unit either counts as a construction or does not. Instead, this approach assumes a gradient scale of constructionhood, understood as the degree to which a pattern is mentally encoded. This view, of course, entails challenges of its own: For example, the question remains of how degrees of constructionhood can be measured and whether such quantification could be used to define a threshold that patterns have to cross to be included in the constructional inventory of a given analysis (see also Section 4.3). However, there are good arguments in favor of a reconceptualization of constructions in gradualist terms – for instance, diachronic studies show very clearly that the emergence of constructions is usually a gradual process (Hartmann 2021; Traugott & Trousdale 2013).

As this discussion has illustrated, the concept of "construction" has undergone a considerable evolution over the last thirty years, and yet researchers are still grappling with its definition and operationalization. The different definitions of the concept have important consequences for the question of which linguistic units can be regarded as constructions – including the question of whether words and morphemes should count as constructions, which is the issue to which we now turn.

2.3 The Lower Boundary: Words and Morphemes as Constructions?

As the preceding sections have shown, Construction Grammarians initially focused on the analysis of idiomatic phrasal constructions such as *let alone*, before extending their purview to more general clause-level patterns like the ditransitive construction. Subsequent research, however, has also applied CxG principles to the "lower" end of the grammatical system, that is, to the lexical and morphological level. One important question in this context is how far "down" the notion of construction extends: Does it include words or even morphemes? We will address this question in two steps, starting with (bound) morphemes and then discussing the status of lexical items. As we shall see, this topic is another example of a seemingly simple question that has given rise to a complex and still ongoing debate.

Starting with the morphological level, some authors have relatively straightforwardly assumed that morphemes are constructions (e.g. Boas 2013; Goldberg 2006). This seems to make intuitive sense for free morphemes that form monomorphemic words such as *car* or *about*. These units match the definitions of "construction" laid out in the previous section: They combine a linguistic form with a meaning, and they are not predictable from other similar items or from their component parts. The same argument has also been made for bound morphemes like *pre-* or *-ing* (Goldberg 2006: 5), which are traditionally regarded as carrying lexical or grammatical meaning. This is, however, where Booij (2010) disagrees: He argues that morphemes should not be regarded as constructions "because morphemes are not linguistic signs, i.e. independent pairings of form and meaning" (Booij 2010: 15). In his view, bound morphemes are not meaningful on their own but only when combined with other items, which is why they are best accounted for by frame-and-slot patterns such as $[[X]_A\text{-}ness]_N$ (as in *greatness*). According to Booij, the latter templates are constructions, but the morphemes that occur in them are not.

Booij's view is appealing, even though one might wonder whether there is really a fundamental difference between regarding bound morphemes as constructions while stipulating that they cannot occur without a base, and positing a morphological construction that combines the morpheme with its (underspecified) base. Perhaps some scholars intend the former option as a shorthand version of the latter: Croft (2001), for example, states that morphemes can be constructions (p. 25), but he simultaneously illustrates them with constructional frames like [NOUN-*s*] (p. 17). Another complication is that the "independence" of a unit (whether it is free or bound) is sometimes difficult to assert, and that the distinction between morphemes and free words may rather be a continuum (Haspelmath 2011). This becomes particularly clear if we look at processes of grammaticalization in which affixes arise from lexical items, as in the development of English -*dom* (e.g. in *kingdom*) from Old English *dom* 'judgment, doom' (Traugott & Trousdale 2013: 170).

Moving on to the lexical level, there is also disagreement about whether words should count as constructions, even though the reasons for this debate are different. On one side of the discussion, some scholars defend a fairly radical version of the lexicon–syntax continuum (see Section 1), according to which words like *apple* are, in terms of their status as constructions, fundamentally the same as clause-level constructions like the ditransitive and differ from the latter only in their degree of abstraction (Hoffmann 2022: 10). In contrast, other researchers (e.g. Dąbrowska 2009; Diessel 2015) have argued that simple words should not be regarded as constructions, while complex words such as *armchair* and *forgetful* should. This is not, however, because these authors do not perceive monomorphemic words as meaningful; rather, they advocate a narrower understanding of the term "construction," restricting it to "grammatical patterns that involve at least two meaningful elements, e.g., two morphemes, words or phrases" (Diessel 2019: 11). Meanwhile, on this view, both simple words and constructions (in the narrow sense) are subsumed under the concept of *signs* in their traditional Saussurean sense as pairings of form and meaning.[4] This understanding of "sign" therefore corresponds to other scholars' use of "construction" in its wide sense – as a result, researchers who adopt the latter view (e.g. Booij 2010; Traugott & Trousdale 2013) often use both terms interchangeably.

The question of whether "sign" or "construction" should serve as the coverall term for the basic units of language may be partly a terminological issue. As Diessel (2019: 11) notes, restricting the term "construction" to complex units echoes its use in traditional grammar (see also Langacker 1987: 83–87). On the other hand, it could be argued that the label "Construction Grammar" implies a wide understanding of the concept, according to which it encompasses the entirety of speakers' grammatical knowledge (in line with Goldberg's

---

[4] The concepts of "sign" and "construction" are also distinguished in Sign-Based CxG (Sag 2012; see Section 3), even though they are used somewhat differently. In this theory, signs correspond to lexemes and fixed multiword expressions; several signs can combine into composite units called "constructs." Meanwhile, "constructions" are descriptions (i.e. sets of constraints) that license constructs, whereas "listemes" license signs.

[2006: 18] claim that "it's constructions all the way down"; see Section 2.2). Terminology aside, however, the deeper underlying question is whether or not there is a fundamental distinction between simple and complex constructions (or, using the alternative terms, between lexical and constructional signs). Diessel (2019: 11) argues that such a distinction is indeed crucial because "lexemes and constructions are learned and processed in very different ways." According to his view (Diessel 2019: 107–111), lexemes are characterized by the fact that they tap directly into speakers' world knowledge and are embedded in rich semantic networks.[5] (Complex) constructions, on the other hand, do not tap directly into encyclopedic knowledge; rather, they provide speakers with "processing instructions" for how lexemes should be combined and interpreted together. Diessel's view also draws support from neurolinguistic evidence suggesting that there are considerable differences in the processing of lexical items compared with units above the word level (Pulvermüller, Cappelle, & Shtyrov 2013).

Nevertheless, the distinction between lexemes and constructions is complicated by several factors. First, the central notion of *complexity* deserves closer attention. At first glance, a complex construction can be relatively easily defined as a pattern that is composed of multiple discernible units or constituents (comparable to the distinction between simplex and complex words; see e.g. Booij 2012: 7). One question, however, is which features of constructions are at issue: Does complexity concern their form or also their meaning? Dąbrowska (2009: 217), for example, taking a Langackerian Cognitive Grammar perspective, argues that relational words such as verbs qualify as constructions because they are complex at both the semantic and the phonological levels. This view rests on the assumption that the semantics of a verb include representations for the participants involved in the event or action encoded by the verb. For example, Dąbrowska suggests that the lexical representation of *trudge* contains representations for the walker and the setting, similar to the more abstract intransitive motion construction, which includes representations for the mover and the path.[6]

---

[5] Note that Diessel's (2019: 11) use of the term "lexemes" also includes morphemes, which is again relevant to the earlier discussion in this section about the status of morphemes as constructions.

[6] This is closely connected to the concept of valency (Tesnière 1959), that is, the capability of linguistic units to combine with different "actants," which has started to gain increasing attention in CxG. The complex ways in which the valency of individual verbs interacts with the constructions in which they occur (Goldberg 1995) casts some more doubt on the strict division between the lexical and the constructional level. Several scholars have indeed argued that a constructionist approach to language can be fruitfully combined with a theory of valency (see e.g. Herbst 2007, 2011; Stefanowitsch 2011).

Another challenge for the distinction between simple and complex linguistic units is that words differ in their degree of analyzability, as has been convincingly demonstrated in the psycholinguistic literature (Hay 2003; Hay & Baayen 2002). This has ramifications not only for their production and processing but also for their phonetic realization (Bell, Ben Hadia, & Plag 2021) and even for the occurrence of spelling variants (Gahl & Plag 2019). For instance, a word like *discernment* can be segmented more readily than a word like *government* (Hay 2003: 136). This can be explained by assuming that complex words lead a "double existence" as instances of a (morphological) construction on the one hand and as lexical items in their own right on the other. The same has been argued for phrasal idioms such as *pull strings*, which seem to be simultaneously analyzed into their component parts and processed holistically (Bybee 1998: 424–425). The fact that expressions can thus be perceived as simple and complex at the same time, and that they may vary in how strongly they lean toward one pole or the other, suggests that the distinction between lexemes and complex constructions may be more gradient than is sometimes assumed.

Summing up, there seem to be arguments both in favor of and against drawing a distinction between simple and complex signs, and consequently between a wide and a narrow use of the term "construction." While this casts doubt on radical conceptions that do not assume any qualitative differences between lexical and grammatical (or syntactic) constructions, it does not invalidate the idea that lexicon and grammar form opposite ends of a continuum. Regarding the question of what counts as a construction, these findings also support the idea of reconceptualizing constructionhood as a gradient and dynamic notion that can accommodate a range of construction types that behave in potentially dissimilar ways.

2.4 Summary

In this section, we have given a brief historical overview of the evolution of constructionist approaches, focusing on the key concept of construction itself. We have reviewed several definitions of constructions, arguing for a gradient and dynamic notion of constructionhood that is also compatible with the most recent definition of constructions proposed by Goldberg (2019). We have also sketched out some ongoing controversies about what types of linguistic units should be seen as constructions. In particular, the jury is still out regarding the question of whether words and morphemes can be considered constructions.

An aspect that we have not yet addressed is to what extent the theoretical disagreements about the definition of constructions affect scholars' daily research practice. In some cases, the practical ramifications for linguistic analyses may be arguably quite limited: For example, researchers can use similar constructionist principles to account for lexical and morphological processes without agreeing on the exact definitions of terms like "construction" and "sign." This may also explain why constructionist scholars can have very compatible views of language and still continue to debate the exact nature of these key concepts.

3 From Sign-Based to Radical: "Flavors" of Construction Grammar

The present Element could have been called *Construction Grammar*. But as CxG has developed into a highly diverse field, it has become quite common to follow, for instance, Goldberg (2013) in speaking of "constructionist approaches." It is, of course, not always possible to tell different approaches clearly apart, nor to allocate individual researchers to a specific constructionist framework. After all, CxG is a very dynamic field of research that takes a bottom-up rather than a top-down approach to language, which entails that many details concerning its theoretical foundations are continually in flux. Nevertheless, we can distinguish different types of CxG along some key parameters. Ziem and Lasch (2013), for example, propose a coarse-grained distinction between formal constructionist approaches, on the one hand, and cognitive, usage-based, and typologically oriented approaches, on the other. Among the formal approaches are Berkeley CxG (Fillmore et al. 1988), Sign-Based CxG (Sag 2012), Fluid CxG (Steels 2011) and Embodied CxG (Bergen & Chang 2005).[7] Meanwhile, the main frameworks that fall into the other (less formal) group are Cognitive CxG (e.g. Goldberg 1995) and Radical CxG (Croft 2001).[8] We cannot give an extensive overview of each of those different approaches here – for more in-depth introductions to the individual frameworks, we refer the reader to the excellent summaries that already exist (see e.g. the contributions in Hoffmann & Trousdale 2013 and the further references in Table 1 in Section 3.4). Instead, we will discuss some important commonalities and differences between the six above-mentioned approaches, focusing on three key areas: formalization, research foci and methods. We will address these

---

[7] Note that, for ease of reading, we use partial abbreviations (e.g. Sign-Based CxG) in the following rather than the full acronyms (in this case, SBCG) that are otherwise common.

[8] We focus here on six major frameworks that have explicitly assumed the label "CxG." We do not discuss Langacker's (1987, 2008) Cognitive Grammar in detail, even though the framework shares many of its assumptions with (especially usage-based) CxG and is sometimes regarded as a type of CxG (e.g. Langacker 2005). We also cannot address the Parallel Architecture (Jackendoff 2002; Jackendoff & Audring 2020). Furthermore, the limited space here does not allow us to discuss a few of the lesser-known constructionist approaches, such as Dynamic CxG (Dominey et al. 2017), Template CxG (Barrès 2017), and Utterance CxG (Cienki 2017).

aspects in turn, considering in particular the more recent developments that have taken place in each framework.

3.1 Formalization

Even though all constructionist approaches employ some degree of formalization, a rough distinction can be drawn between approaches that use more elaborate and strictly defined formal conventions and those that do not. As mentioned at the beginning of Section 3, Berkeley, Sign-Based, Fluid, and Embodied CxG can be counted among the more formal frameworks, while Cognitive and Radical CxG constitute less formal variants.

The formal Construction Grammars share two important characteristics. First, they represent constructions in the form of feature structures, and more specifically as *attribute-value matrices (AVMs)*. Each construction is characterized by a number of syntactic attributes, for example syntactic category and valence, and semantic attributes, such as reference and thematic roles; each of these attributes is assigned a unique value. This is illustrated in Figure 1 with a Sign-Based CxG analysis of the subject–predicate construction, which licenses basic declarative clauses (Michaelis 2013). As the diagram shows, the construction specifies two daughters that combine into a mother node. The head daughter *H*, in this case the verb, is defined by several syntactic features: its category (finite verb), its valents (the other daughter *X*, here the subject), and its marking (i.e. the absence of a grammatical marker such as the complementizer *that*). The mother node is similarly unmarked, and has an empty valence list because it selects no further arguments. Naturally, specific frameworks vary somewhat in terms of the attributes they use and how flexibly they handle them. Especially the computationally oriented approaches, Fluid CxG and Embodied CxG, tend to be relatively agnostic regarding what specific features should be included in the representations, as long as they improve the performance of the models (Steels 2017: 188).

The second hallmark of formal Construction Grammars concerns the specific mechanism they use to combine feature structures: *unification*.

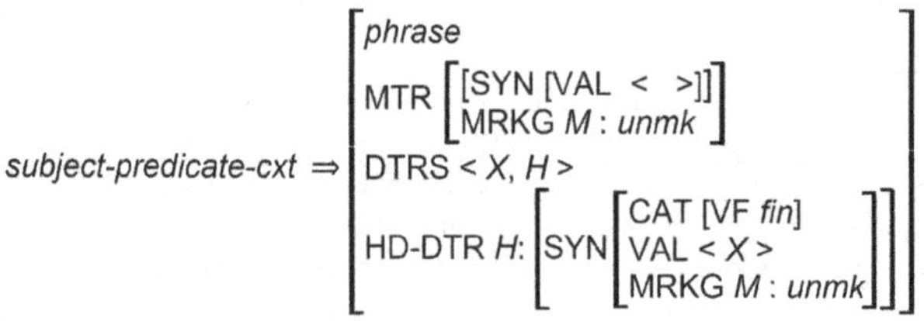

$$
\text{subject-predicate-cxt} \Rightarrow
\begin{bmatrix}
phrase \\
\text{MTR} \begin{bmatrix} \text{[SYN [VAL < >]]} \\ \text{MRKG } M : unmk \end{bmatrix} \\
\text{DTRS} < X, H > \\
\text{HD-DTR } H: \begin{bmatrix} \text{SYN} \begin{bmatrix} \text{CAT [VF } fin] \\ \text{VAL} < X > \\ \text{MRKG } M : unmk \end{bmatrix} \end{bmatrix}
\end{bmatrix}
$$

Figure 1 Sign-Based CxG formalism: a feature-based analysis of the subject–predicate construction (reproduced from Michaelis 2013: 142)

This operation has played a long-standing role in constraint-based theories such as Gazdar et al.'s (1985) Generalized Phrase Structure Grammar (GPSG) and Pollard and Sag's (1987) Head-Driven Phrase Structure Grammar (HPSG), both of which heavily inspired Sign-Based CxG (see Michaelis 2015: 151). Unification is defined as an operation by which two structures that have matching feature values combine into a new structure that "contains no more and no less than what is contained in its component AVMs" (Fried & Östman 2004: 33; see also Shieber 1986). For example, returning to the example in Figure 1, the verb unifies with an argument that matches its valence specification in order to form a subject–predicate phrase.

In contrast to the aforementioned approaches, the less formal Construction Grammars – Cognitive CxG and Radical CxG – use neither AVM-style feature structures nor unification. The lack of formalism in these approaches is intentional, as Goldberg (2013: 29) highlights: "I have avoided using all but the most minimal formalization in my own work because I believe the necessary use of features that formalism requires misleads researchers into believing that there might be a finite list of features or that many or most of the features are valid in cross-linguistic work. The facts belie this implication."

Goldberg (2006: 216–217) provides several further arguments against the use of AVMs for representing constructions. For example, she remarks that formalist approaches often do not account for the rich frame semantics of constructions and instead describe their semantic features in terms of simple "constants." Moreover, she argues that formal analyses tend to overemphasize syntactic features over semantic ones, and that the formalisms are usually too unwieldy to capture the amount and complexity of speakers' constructional knowledge. Finally, the aforementioned quote from Goldberg (2013) also questions the typological validity of the features used in formal approaches, a theme that is particularly prominent in Croft's Radical CxG. Croft (2001, 2020) argues against the universality of grammatical categories such as word classes (e.g. noun, adjective) and syntactic relations (e.g. subject, object). Based on evidence from typologically distant languages, he shows that both the syntactic environments that define word classes and the linking mechanisms between verbs and their arguments vary considerably across languages. As a result, he suggests that word classes are characterized by language-specific constructions and that syntactic relations can be derived from underlying semantic relations (again, in construction-specific ways).

It is debatable whether Goldberg's and Croft's criticisms – also considering that some of them were stated a while ago – still paint an accurate picture of formal Construction Grammars, and if so, how the problems they identify could be resolved. For one, some of the authors' remarks have been accommodated by the formal approaches: Features, for example, can have complex values, so the semantic attributes of AVMs can be filled by rich semantic frames, a practice that has been adopted in recent formal work (Sag 2012; Steels 2017). It also seems feasible that the features posited by these frameworks could be defined in language-specific ways rather than via universal primitives, thus accounting for typological variability in their realization (see e.g. Fried & Östman 2004: 77).

Another question is whether the less formal varieties of CxG deal more successfully with the challenges identified by Goldberg and Croft. While nonformal Construction Grammars typically do not rely on elaborate feature structures, they nevertheless characterize constructions in terms of their salient properties. Compare Figure 2, which reproduces a Cognitive CxG analysis of the ditransitive construction (Goldberg 2006; see Section 2.2 for examples). The upper half of the diagram outlines the semantic properties of the construction (its overall meaning and the thematic roles it comprises), while the lower half specifies its syntactic functions. Other researchers working in nonformal Construction Grammars have used even more abbreviated representations, such as the bracketed notation in (8). Nevertheless, both these representations comprise the same features that could also be listed as part of an AVM (e.g. as a valence list or within a semantic frame). It is also worth noting that Figure 2 makes use of the same grammatical categories (e.g. syntactic functions) that Croft (2000, 2021) criticizes for their lack of crosslinguistic validity. While these categories may not be crosslinguistically stable, it appears that, for the purposes of a language-specific analysis, they provide a useful and ultimately indispensable way of capturing generalizations.

(8)   [[SUBJ V OBJ1 OBJ2] ↔ [X CAUSE Y to RECEIVE Z]] (Traugott & Trousdale 2013: 59)

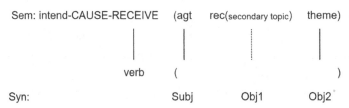

Figure 2 Cognitive CxG analysis of the ditransitive construction
(reproduced from Goldberg 2006: 20)

All things considered, there may be no principled reasons why Construction Grammars should or should not rely on a certain degree of formalization. Rather, it seems that the differences between frameworks are largely a result of their specific research goals (which will be discussed in more detail in the next section). For example, a primary goal of Sign-Based CxG and related formal approaches is to account for "the licensing of word strings by rules of syntactic and semantic composition" (Michaelis 2015: 151) – an enterprise that these frameworks share with traditional generative grammar. For this purpose, it seems feasible to employ a rigorous unification-based formalism that captures how well-formed structures arise from feature matching among their component parts. Moreover, unification lends itself to computational implementation (Knight 1989); and the algorithms are not affected by how detailed and potentially "unwieldy" the AVMs are. For the less formal Construction Grammars, on the other hand, the readability of the representations is an important consideration, and researchers tend to highlight only those features of constructions that are relevant for their respective analyses. For the purposes of the latter – which focus on the mental representation of constructions and their use in naturalistic speech – the use of precise formalisms may thus be less important.

3.2 Research Foci

As hinted at in Section 3.1, the different "flavors" of CxG are not only distinguished by their degree of formalization, but they also differ in terms of the research questions they tend to emphasize. Broadly, three subgroups can be distinguished in this context, characterized by their respective focus on (i) grammatical description; (ii) computational modeling; or (iii) the cognitive and typological dimensions of language use.

Starting with the first group, Berkeley CxG and its successor framework, Sign-Based CxG, have primarily been concerned with providing detailed descriptions of grammatical phenomena, using the formal tools discussed in the previous section. As outlined in Section 2.1, the early work by the Berkeley group focused particularly on analyses of partially filled idioms, such as *let alone* (Fillmore et al. 1988) and the *What's X doing Y?* construction (Kay & Fillmore 1999). This interest was soon extended to constructions in other languages that carry specific syntactic, semantic, or pragmatic properties, such as right-detached *comme* in French, as in *C'est cher, comme appareil, ça* 'That's an expensive camera' (Lambrecht 2004). Moreover, proponents of the framework have also investigated more general, nonidiomatic phenomena, such as extraposition (Michaelis & Lambrecht 1996) and different verb-complementation patterns (Fillmore 2013).

This line of research has been carried on by Sign-Based CxG, which was partially developed by proponents of the earlier Berkeley approach. In his detailed overview of the paradigm, Sag (2012) provides Sign-Based analyses of a broad range of construction types, including lexical classes (e.g. the main verb construction), inflectional morphology (e.g. the preterite construction), phrasal structure (e.g. the head-complement construction), and argument structure (e.g. the ditransitive). It has been suggested that Sign-Based CxG tends to focus more on the formal-syntactic rather than the semantic aspects of constructions (e.g. Feldman 2020: 151). For example, to account for filler-gap phenomena such as *wh*-interrogatives and topicalization, Sag (2010) posits an overarching construction that only has formal specifications but no meaning. This contrasts with other views, primarily by proponents of Cognitive CxG, who have called the existence of meaningless schemas into question, arguing instead that every construction must have a meaning, even if only a highly abstract one (Goldberg 2006: 166–182; Hilpert 2019: 50–74; Sommerer and Baumann 2021: 125–126).

Moving on to the second group of theories that share an overall research goal, Fluid CxG and Embodied CxG aim primarily at constructing computational models of language processing. As a result, the two frameworks focus particularly on the practical challenges involved in creating functional CxG implementations. Still, the two approaches differ somewhat in terms of their backgrounds and research foci. Fluid CxG has been under development at computer science labs in Paris and Brussels since the late 1990s. Its main goal is to create a construction-based architecture for language production and comprehension (Steels 2017). In doing so, the proponents of the framework "do not make any claims about biological realism or cognitive relevance" (Steels 2017: 181), focusing instead on maximizing the descriptive coverage of their models. Recent analyses have addressed a range of constructions, including English auxiliaries (Van Trijp 2017) and long-distance dependencies (Van Trijp 2014), Dutch word order (Van Eecke 2017), and Spanish verb conjugation (Beuls 2017). Moreover, the approach has been used to model aspects of language evolution (Steels 2012; Steels & Szathmáry 2016). In parallel to these research contributions, Fluid CxG has generated a number of real-world applications, among them a model for visual question answering (i.e. answering text questions about images; Nevens, Eecke, & Beuls 2019) and a platform for analyzing opinions on social media (Willaert et al. 2020).

Embodied CxG, on the other hand, developed out of the Neural Theory of Language project (Feldman 2006) at the University of California, Berkeley. As a result, its proponents aim to model speakers' grammatical processing specifically in relation to its neural underpinnings. In contrast to the other formally oriented Construction Grammars, Embodied CxG emphasizes the analysis of meaning, and of embodied meaning in particular (Feldman 2020: 151). As Bergen and Chang (2013) outline, the framework aims to account for the role of embodied simulation in language processing, that is, speakers' tendency to activate perceptual and motor systems in the brain that recreate experiences similar to the ones that arise during actual perception or movement (Barsalou 1999). Previous studies have used Embodied CxG to analyze phenomena such as the English caused-motion construction (Dodge & Petruck 2014) and Hebrew verbal morphology (Schneider 2010), and to model aspects of grammatical parsing (Bryant 2008) and acquisition (Mok 2009). Recent work, meanwhile, has somewhat moved away from linguistic analysis and instead focused on technological applications in natural language understanding, including verbal control of robots (Eppe et al. 2016) and a system for providing health advice (Feldman 2020).

Finally, as a third group that is characterized by similar research goals, Cognitive CxG and Radical CxG focus on the cognitive, typological, and contextual factors that underlie and shape speakers' grammatical knowledge. In contrast to the above-mentioned frameworks, these approaches identify themselves as "usage-based" (see e.g. Barlow & Kemmer 2000; Langacker 1988; Tomasello 2003), devoting their attention to how "experience with language creates and impacts the cognitive representations for language" (Bybee 2013: 49). As a result, the frameworks are sometimes grouped under the broader label of "Usage-Based CxG" (e.g. Diessel 2015).[9] Compared with the other approaches discussed above, proponents of usage-based Construction Grammars tend to focus less on the form side of constructions and more on characterizing their rich meanings in psychologically plausible ways, using concepts such as construal (Langacker 2019), conceptual blending (Turner 2019), and semantic maps for cross-linguistic comparisons (Croft 2022).

Despite their similarities, Cognitive and Radical CxG also differ in terms of their research questions. Proponents of Cognitive CxG are particularly concerned with how constructions motivate each other in virtue of their mutual similarities and associative relations (Booij 2017; Goldberg 1995; Lakoff 1987), a notion that is captured by positing networks of constructions (see Section 4 for a detailed discussion). In addition, they often study how speakers' linguistic behavior is shaped by domain-general cognitive processes such as attention,

---

[9] A reviewer points out that early work in Cognitive CxG can be considered less usage-based than current approaches, as it did not really capture the dynamic view of grammar that characterizes the usage-based approach, and instead relied on concepts like inheritance that can be traced back to more formal approaches to grammar. On this view, Cognitive CxG has experienced a "usage-based turn."

categorization, analogy, and social cognition (e.g. Bybee 2013; Diessel 2019; Goldberg 2019). As what is probably the largest strand of CxG to date, Cognitive CxG has spawned an extensive body of work. While the paradigm became initially known particularly for its analyses of argument-structure constructions (e.g. Boas 2003; Goldberg 1995; Perek 2015), its proponents have since tackled a wide range of other phenomena, including (but not limited to) complex clauses (Hoffmann 2011), information structure (Goldberg 2005), discourse organization (Traugott 2022), tense and modality (Bergs 2010; Cappelle & Depraetere 2016), and phrase-internal structure (Sommerer 2018), as well as inflectional and derivational morphology (Booij 2010). The framework is also often extended to diachrony, with many proponents of "Diachronic Construction Grammar" (Coussé, Andersson, & Olofsson 2018; Sommerer & Smirnova 2020; Traugott & Trousdale 2013) situating their work broadly within Goldbergian usage-based CxG (see Section 4.1 for an explanation of key diachronic concepts such as "constructionalization"). Moreover, there has been considerable research on language acquisition, focusing in particular on children's early item-based constructions (e.g. ___ *gone*, as in *Cherry gone*; Tomasello 1992), the emergence of abstract constructions, and the acquisition of complex sentences (for overviews, see Behrens 2021; Diessel 2013; Tomasello 2003).

Radical CxG, on the other hand, relies on a smaller body of work, most of it created by William Croft (e.g. 2001; 2020). The framework has a strong typological focus, centering on the question of which aspects of speakers' grammatical knowledge are language- and construction-specific, and which ones may be universal. In his work, Croft discusses many grammatical core phenomena, including word classes, argument structure, syntactic roles, and grammatical categories like voice, aspect, and tense. Further applications have extended the framework to aspects of grammar acquisition (Deuchar and Vihman 2005) and template-based phonology (Vihman & Croft 2007) as well as modal and discourse particles (Fischer & Alm 2013).

3.3 Methods

Across the different constructionist approaches, there is a broad consensus that in order to understand the nature and use of constructions, we need evidence from a wide variety of sources – more technically, we have to *triangulate* evidence from different methodological approaches (Baker & Egbert 2016). Still, we can draw some broad generalizations in terms of which methods the different approaches are most closely connected to.

First, it should be acknowledged that all types of CxG rely to some extent on the "introspective" method, that is, researchers' use of their own intuitive judgments to analyze selected examples and develop theoretical accounts (but see Willems 2012 for potential differences between introspection and intuition). Introspection plays a crucial role in all theoretical and descriptive approaches to grammar: As Janda (2013: 6) points out, "[i]ntrospection is irreplaceable in the descriptive documentation of language" (see also Talmy 2007). While many Construction Grammarians, especially proponents of the more usage-based varieties, are skeptical of introspection, perceiving it perhaps as a hallmark of more traditional (generative) analyses (Willems 2012: 665), the method nevertheless serves an important role in hypothesis generation, theory building, and the interpretation of results.

Beyond that, most Construction Grammarians agree that introspection needs to be combined with other sources of evidence, but specific approaches differ in terms of what methods they use and the extent to which they apply them. Naturally, the choice of methods is closely related to the research goals of the different frameworks. As such, Berkeley and Sign-Based CxG tend to rely relatively strongly on fine-grained theoretical analyses, in line with their goal of providing a formally rigorous account of the grammatical system. Nevertheless, work in these areas has also been partially assisted by corpus methods – see, for example, Brenier and Michaelis (2005) for a corpus-based study of copula doubling in the context of formal CxG.

Especially Cognitive CxG has developed a broad inventory of empirical methods to study the synchronic and diachronic use of constructions and draw inferences about their representation in speakers' minds. In particular, proponents of the framework draw on an ever-expanding set of corpus-based methods. These approaches are guided by the usage-based assumption that linguistic knowledge is experience-based: Children learn language by detecting patterns in the input they receive, thus building up a dynamic network of constructions that is subject to lifelong reorganization (Ambridge & Lieven 2011; Taylor 2012; Tomasello 2003). In line with this, constructionist corpus analyses aim at gauging language users' linguistic knowledge on the basis of frequency and distribution data from authentic usage. They draw primarily on measures of frequency, dispersion, and association (Divjak 2019; Gries 2008), distributional semantic methods (Hilpert & Perek 2015; Perek 2016), and (most recently) artificial neural networks (Budts 2022; Budts & Petré 2020).

One particularly widespread corpus-based method in constructionist work is collostructional analysis (Gries & Stefanowitsch 2004; Stefanowitsch & Gries 2003, 2005). Following a long tradition of corpus-linguistic approaches that investigate collocations, that is, words that occur together, collostructional analysis focuses on the interaction between words and constructions. Consider, for instance, the *into*-causative construction, as in *They talked us into writing this*

Element: Using the simplest version of collostructional analysis, simple collexeme analysis, Stefanowitsch and Gries (2003: 225) show that words like *trick, fool,* and *coerce* occur at above-chance level in the first verb slot of this construction, when compared to their total corpus frequency. Using covarying collexeme analysis, which focuses on the co-occurrence of items in a construction with two open slots, Stefanowitsch and Gries (2005: 13) furthermore show that *fool* and *thinking* are most likely to occur together in the construction, while other verb pairs like *force into thinking* or *provoke into accepting* are much less likely to co-occur. Importantly, collostructional techniques are also subject to constant refinement, as their methodological rationale and cognitive underpinnings have been controversially, and sometimes heatedly, debated (Gries 2015; Küchenhoff & Schmid 2015; Schmid & Küchenhoff 2013).

These corpus approaches have come to be increasingly complemented by experimental paradigms, which are used especially by proponents of Cognitive CxG but also inform research in other frameworks such as Fluid and Embodied CxG (e.g. Bergen 2007; Feldman 2006). Commonly used methods include acceptability judgments (Dąbrowska 2008; Gries & Wulff 2009), sorting tasks (Bencini & Goldberg 2000; Perek 2012), artificial language learning (Casenhiser & Goldberg 2005; Perek & Goldberg 2015), priming (Busso, Perek, & Lenci, 2021; Ungerer 2021, 2022), and a number of other techniques, such as sentence repetition (Diessel & Tomasello 2005) and sentence completion (Perek 2015). Experimental approaches are needed because many aspects related to the processing, storage, and acquisition of constructions cannot be satisfactorily answered on the basis of corpus data alone. Among other things, experimental studies have lent support to the cognitive reality of "constructions" as meaningful elements of speakers' linguistic knowledge. Bencini and Goldberg (2000), for example, presented speakers with a list of sentences that differed either in terms of the verb they contained or the construction they instantiated, and asked participants to sort the sentences into categories. Interestingly, the authors found that participants were more likely to group instances of the same construction into a category than sentences with the same verb. This suggests that constructions are psychologically real units that play an important role for the way speakers categorize the linguistic input.

Meanwhile, artificial language-learning experiments can shed light on how the input shapes speakers' acquisition of new constructions. In Perek and Goldberg's (2015) study, for example, participants were exposed to made-up verbs (e.g. *moop*) that occurred in novel constructions (featuring non-English word orders). Depending on whether the verbs combined with different constructions or always with the same construction during the training phase, participants used them either more "liberally" or more "conservatively" in a subsequent productive task, suggesting that the input determined what constructional generalizations speakers formed. Finally, priming studies are particularly informative about relations between constructions in speakers' mental networks. This follows from the assumption that the degree to which one construction primes, that is, affects the processing of, another construction functions as an indicator of how similar speakers' representations of the two patterns are (Ungerer 2022; see Section 4.1 for details).

While constructionist research has thus drawn on a variety of experimental methods, the paradigm could further benefit from other techniques used in the wider context of cognitive linguistics, especially in experimental semantics (Matlock & Winter 2015) and experimental semiotics (Nölle & Galantucci 2023). Research in the former field, which investigates the meaning not only of individual words but also of constructions, has obvious implications for constructionist work. For example, using a mouse-tracking paradigm, Anderson, Matlock, and Spivery (2013) found interesting differences between sentences with varying aspectual construal (progressive vs. nonprogressive), thus supporting the cognitive-linguistic hypothesis that distinct grammatical constructions yield differences in semantic construal. Experimental semiotics, meanwhile, addresses the question of how symbolic systems come about by conducting laboratory studies that involve novel communication systems. For instance, Goldin-Meadow et al. (2008) and Christensen, Fusaroli and Tylén (2016) used silent-gesture paradigms to account for the emergence and cognitive underpinnings of cross-linguistically well-attested word-order preferences. Especially for usage-based CxG, which sees language as a highly dynamic system, the results of these studies are particularly relevant because they can help explain common pathways of language change and grammaticalization (or "constructionalization"; see Section 4.1).

Returning to other methods used in CxG, constructionist work in the Berkeley tradition has given rise to a research strand that we have not addressed so far and which uses lexicographic methods to build large-scale repositories of constructions. Researchers working in this area, which has become known as "constructicography" (Lyngfelt et al. 2018), create construction entries that are then linked up with semantic frames from FrameNet (Fillmore et al. 2012). A semantic frame is here defined as "any system of concepts related in such a way that to understand any one concept it is necessary to understand the entire system" (Petruck 2022: 592). Constructional inventories, or "construct-i-cons" (see Section 4), are currently being built for several languages, including English (Perek & Patten 2019), German (Ziem, Flick, & Sandkühler 2019), Russian (Janda et al. 2018), and Brazilian Portuguese (Torrent et al. 2018). While such constructional inventories can form the basis for cross-linguistic comparisons, the strand of CxG that has most strongly focused on comparative methods is arguably Radical CxG. Notably, proponents of this paradigm often rely on qualitative analyses rather than quantitative tools (but see e.g. Deuchar & Vihman 2005 for quantitative case studies of language acquisition from a Radical CxG perspective).

Finally, the methods discussed so far are complemented by computational approaches, which are used in particular by Fluid and Embodied CxG to model aspects of language comprehension and/or production. Fluid CxG provides what is arguably the most advanced computational implementation of CxG to date. The use of this formalism has been recently facilitated by the release of the FCG Editor (Van Trijp, Beuls, & Van Eecke 2022), an open-source development tool with which researchers can customize their own grammars for sentence parsing and production. Proponents of Fluid CxG have also created models of language learning and evolution using autonomous robots that play language games (Steels & Hild 2012). Embodied CxG, meanwhile, has developed its own development platform, the ECG workbench (Eppe et al. 2016), even though the latter seems to have more limited functionality than its Fluid CxG counterpart (Van Trijp et al. 2022: 6–7).

3.4 Summary

In this section, we have provided a brief sketch of the six major variants of CxG, focusing on their similarities and differences in terms of formalization, research goals, and methods. The results of our comparisons are summarized in Table 1. Of course, the broad generalizations we have outlined are limited in several ways: They cannot do justice to the whole body of work in the respective areas, nor is it always possible to decide which specific framework a certain contribution should be attributed to. For example, the constructicography projects described in Section 3.3 (i.e. the creation of language-specific constructional inventories) stand in the tradition of Berkeley-style frame semantics, but they also share elements with other constructionist approaches, for example with respect to their usage-based orientation and the use of data-driven methods. Such overlap across frameworks is to be expected: After all, CxG is an eclectic and constantly developing field, whose proponents share many of their core assumptions and thus often enter into fruitful collaborations.

4 Connecting the Dots: The Construct-i-con

Despite the differences that exist between specific constructionist frameworks, as discussed in the previous section, all Construction Grammarians agree on certain fundamental assumptions. One of these ideas – that language comes in

Table 1 Summary of similarities and differences among the six "flavors" of Construction Grammar

	Berkeley CxG	Sign-Based CxG	Fluid CxG	Embodied CxG	Cognitive CxG	Radical CxG
Formalization	High degree of formalization, characterized by attribute value matrices (AVMs)				Limited formalization with varying notations (e.g. boxes, brackets)	
Research foci	Grammatical description, both of idiomatic and "regular" constructions; focus on constructional form		Computational modeling of language comprehension and/or production; language learning and evolution; technological applications		Cognitive and typological dimensions of language use; usage-based orientation; focus on constructional meaning; language change and acquisition	
Methods	Introspective analysis; some empirical (corpus-based) work; constructicography		Introspective analysis; computational modeling (using customized software); psycholinguistic and neurolinguistic evidence		Introspective analysis; extensive corpus-based work; experimental methods	Introspective analysis; (largely qualitative) cross-linguistic comparisons
Core references	Fillmore (2013); Fillmore et al. (1988); Fried and Östman (2004)	Boas and Sag (2012); Michaelis (2013, 2015)	Steels (2011, 2013, 2017); Van Trijp et al. (2022)	Bergen and Chang (2005, 2013); Feldman, Dodge, and Bryant (2015); Feldman (2020)	Boas (2013); Goldberg (1995, 2006, 2019); Hilpert (2019)	Croft (2001, 2013, 2020)

the format of form–meaning pairings, or constructions – was introduced in Section 2. Here we discuss a second core tenet: namely that constructions do not exist in isolation from each other, but that rather their forms and meanings are intricately interconnected. To account for these relationships, Construction Grammarians model language as a *network* of constructions stored within speakers' minds (e.g. Booij 2010; Bybee 2010; Diessel 2019, 2023; Fried & Östman 2004; Goldberg 1995, 2019; Sommerer & Smirnova 2020; Traugott & Trousdale 2013). Positing such a constructional network, also known as a *construct-i-con* (or "constructicon"), marks another radical departure from mainstream generative grammar: Rather than assuming that speakers derive grammatical patterns "on the fly" based on abstract principles and procedural rules, the constructionist view is that speakers store a vast inventory of linguistic units, including morphemes and words as well as phrase- and clause-level structures, as part of their long-term declarative knowledge.[10]

In the following sections, we will first discuss some key characteristics of the network model, before taking a closer look at the different types of network relations that have been proposed. We will then outline some further questions and open research problems that concern the architecture of constructional networks and the way in which they can be investigated.

4.1 The Network Model: Characteristics and Applications

Modeling language as a network captures the basic insight that words and complex constructions do not exist in isolation but share varying types of relations with each other. Consider the example of the ditransitive construction in (9a). By combining the words of the example into phrases (e.g. *the* and *student* into the subject), and those phrases (the subject, verb, and two objects) into a sentence, speakers naturally establish relationships between the smaller units. Construction Grammarians typically refer to these links between linearly co-occurring units as *syntagmatic relations* (alternatively known as *sequential relations*; Diessel 2019). These relations can be captured in a network in which words (or phrases) are linked to their frequently co-occurring neighbors.

(9)   a. The student gave his friend the lecture notes.
         b. The student gave the lecture notes to his friend.

---

[10] It should be noted that the view of linguistic knowledge as a network is not unique to CxG, but that it is also a central feature of other cognitively oriented theories such as Cognitive Grammar (Langacker 1987), the Parallel Architecture (Jackendoff 2002), and Word Grammar (Hudson 2007). Within the context of the latter, for instance, Hudson (2015: 692) argues that language is "networks all the way down" (thus adapting Goldberg's [2006] well-known slogan). Moreover, several key notions discussed in this section, such as inheritance hierarchies, also play an important role in other constraint-based frameworks like Head-Driven Phrase Structure Grammar (HPSG; Pollard & Sag 1987).

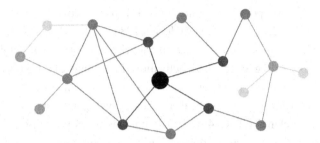

Figure 3 Schematic network diagram

Meanwhile, the example in (9a) also has other types of "relatives": For example, it shares a relation of similarity with the *to*-dative example in (9b). The *to*-dative is usually interpreted as the alternating, that is, near-synonymous, counterpart of the ditransitive construction (Perek 2015; but see Pijpops 2020 for the varying meanings of "alternation"). Based on their similarity, the two patterns can be substituted along the paradigmatic axis, that is, they can fill the same position in a piece of discourse. As a result, they can be modeled as units in a network that are linked via a *paradigmatic relation*.

Networks are a powerful tool for capturing diverse kinds of relations between elements. As such, they have been increasingly used to analyze complex phenomena across the natural and social sciences (Buchanan 2002). Network science – the interdisciplinary study of networks – has been heralded by some as the "science of the 21st century" (Barabási 2016: 25). Figure 3 illustrates the key features of network representations with the help of a schematic diagram. Networks consist of nodes (or vertices) and links (or edges), both of which can represent a variety of things. In the case of constructional networks, nodes can correspond to different linguistic units, such as morphemes, words, or complex constructions. Similarly, the links can instantiate varying relations, such as the syntagmatic and paradigmatic relations introduced above (see Section 4.2 for further linking types), even though researchers often restrict their analyses to one linking type only. Moreover, scholars sometimes use alternative graphic means to draw their diagrams, for example by using annotated boxes for the nodes and arrows for the links (if the network relations are directed).

Grammatical networks, as they are envisaged by Construction Grammarians, are situated in the minds of speakers. As such, they are directly involved in the storage and retrieval of information during the processing of linguistic utterances. Figure 3 provides some additional clues as to how such processing may operate within the network (see also Diessel 2019; Langacker 2017; Schmid 2020 for discussion). The large circle in the center of the diagram represents the construction that is activated during a particular usage event; this construction serves as an "entry point" (Schmid 2020: 44) to the network. Following the principle of spreading activation (Anderson 1983; Collins & Loftus 1975), the currently active unit is then assumed to trigger the activation of neighboring network units, leading to a chain of activation. These units can, for instance, be frequently co-occurring lexical items or constructions, or items that are related in virtue of their similarity (see the discussion of syntagmatic and paradigmatic links above). Schmid (2020: 46), for example, assumes that different mental states representing the same communicative goal are connected via associations – a form like *the boy*, then, would trigger (near-)synonyms like *the young man, the teenager*, and so on. The strength of activation a unit receives from another depends on how closely the two are related; with increasing distance in the network, the amount of activation spread decays. This is illustrated by the grayscale of the nodes and links in Figure 3, where fainter shades represent increasingly lower activation levels.

This brief outline of the network model hints at several reasons for why networks have acquired such a central role in CxG research. First, the network model is naturally compatible with a number of frequently observed psychological effects, both providing a framework for interpreting these effects and drawing additional empirical support from them. Among the phenomena discussed by Diessel (2019: 201–202) and Schmid (2020: 53–55) are: (i) frequency effects, that is, the tendency for more frequent units to be recognized faster and more accurately, which can be explained via their increased resting activation in the network; (ii) recency effects, that is, the tendency for recently activated units to be recognized faster, which can be attributed to their residual activation in the network; and (iii) neighborhood effects, that is, slower recognition of units in dense network neighborhoods, which is likely to arise from competition among co-activated patterns. Related to recency effects, another pervasive phenomenon is priming, defined as a change in speakers' response to a stimulus after previous exposure to the same or a similar item (Branigan & Pickering 2017: 6). Priming occurs both at the lexical level – between words that are semantically, phonetically, or orthographically related (Goldinger, Luce, & Pisoni 1989; Meyer & Schvaneveldt 1971; Meyer, Schvaneveldt, & Ruddy 1974) – and at the level of complex constructions, where the phenomenon is known as "structural priming" (Branigan & Pickering 2017). Regarding the latter, structural priming effects have been observed not only between instances of the same construction (e.g. between two ditransitive sentences; Bock 1986) but also between distinct but related constructions (e.g. between benefactive and dative sentences; Ziegler & Snedeker 2018). As a result, priming effects are regarded as one of the strongest sources of evidence for the network model (Diessel 2019: 204; Ungerer 2021, 2022).

Second, networks provide a dynamic tool for modeling processes of language change. Smirnova and Sommerer (2020: 3) argue that all types of linguistic change can be reconceptualized as network changes, given that the constructional network that makes up a language can change via node creation or loss, via node-internal changes, or via reconfigurations of the network. The creation of a new node roughly corresponds to what Traugott and Trousdale (2013) call *constructionalization*, while the loss of a node can be characterized in terms of constructional attrition (Colleman & Noël 2012), that is, the phenomenon whereby a construction gradually falls out of use. Node-internal changes are roughly equivalent to Traugott and Trousdale's *constructional changes* (but see Smirnova & Sommerer [2020: 9–18], who argue that constructionalization and constructional changes often cannot be clearly told apart). For example, the grammaticalization of a new future marker such as the English *going to* future construction could be described as the emergence of a new node in the constructional network, while the ongoing change of *because*, which used to take only verbal complements and is currently extending its usage domain to nominal complements (*because reasons*), could be considered a node-internal change. Node-internal changes can, in turn, entail the emergence of new nodes and as such lead to a reconfiguration of the constructional network. Lorenz (2020), for instance, demonstrates that the contracted forms *gonna, wanna*, and *gotta* have over time developed their own usage profiles, which are distinct from those of the full forms *going to, want to*, and *got to*.

Another example of a linguistic change that can be conceived of as a reconfiguration in the constructional network is constructional contamination as described by Pijpops and Van de Velde (2016). Constructional contamination occurs when two superficially similar (but unrelated) constructions influence each other. Their example concerns two etymologically and structurally unrelated constructions in Dutch: the partitive genitive, as in *iets verkeerd(s) gegeten* 'eaten something wrong', where a variant with -*s* alternates with an *s*-less variant; and a construction in which the quantifier *iets* 'something' forms an independent noun phrase while *verkeerd* "wrongly" functions as an adverb, as in ... *dat iets verkeerd geïnterpreteerd wordt* '... that something gets wrongly interpreted' (Pijpops & Van de Velde 2016: 544–545). The authors show that the frequent co-occurrence of *iets* and *verkeerd* leads to "a measureable preference for the variant without -*s* in partitive genitives" (Pijpops & Van de Velde 2016: 545). De Smet et al. (2018), meanwhile, discuss how functional relatedness between similar forms can both increase and decrease over time, using the concepts of attraction and differentiation. Attraction means that two forms become more similar to each other over time, which the authors show to be the case for [*begin* + *ing*-clause] and [*begin* + *to*-infinitive]. Differentiation means that two constructions become less similar, which seems to have been the case for [*start* + *ing*-clause] and [*start* + *to*-infinitive]. However, as the authors argue, what looks like differentiation might actually be an epiphenomenon of underlying attraction processes: As [*start* + *to*-infinitive] became increasingly attracted to [*begin* + *to*-infinitive], it became less similar to [*start* + *ing*-clause]. This shows that network changes cannot be studied independently from each other and that the "bigger picture" of the constructional network needs to be taken into account.

4.2 Types of Network Links

A crucial aspect of the network structure that scholars continue to debate concerns the types of links that should be part of the network model. Most Construction Grammarians agree on at least three types of such relations. Two of them were already introduced in Section 4.1: paradigmatic relations between similar units and syntagmatic relations between linearly co-occurring units. A third type consists of *symbolic relations*, which connect the form and the meaning pole of constructions (e.g. Croft 2001; Langacker 1987). By positing these symbolic relations, researchers can use the network model to capture the fundamental CxG view of grammatical units as form–meaning pairings (see Section 2).

While symbolic links seem to be a natural element of the network model, they also pose a potential challenge. If constructional networks are assumed to be "networks of constructions," that is, networks in which constructions function as the nodes then symbolic relations are, strictly speaking, not links between network nodes but part of the nodes themselves. In other words, the nodes in such a model would be internally complex units that consist of a pair of interlinked form and meaning. This view is embraced by Diessel (2019: 11–22), who treats constructions (or "signs," in his terminology) as the basic nodes of the network (which is thus a "network of signs") but also assumes that these nodes themselves consist of networks (i.e. "signs as networks"). The result of this is a "nested" network (see also Diessel 2023) that comprises several layers, with symbolic links only featuring at the construction-internal layer and not at the layer at which different constructions are related to each other (see also Smirnova & Sommerer 2020, who distinguish between a "node-external" and a "node-internal" level). While this offers a possible solution, in practice it means that symbolic links are often not explicitly represented in network diagrams, which tend to focus on the relations between constructions rather than on their internal connectivity.

Returning to the paradigmatic and syntagmatic relations discussed above, these links, too, come with their own complexities. Even though the two linking

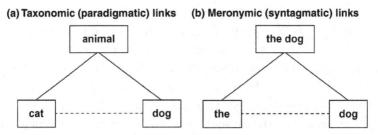

Figure 4 Parallels between taxonomic and meronomic hierarchies, including vertical links (solid lines) and horizontal links (dashed lines)

types encode fundamentally different relations, a crucial feature they share is that they both give rise to hierarchical organization. Specifically, paradigmatically related units form *taxonomies*, that is, series of increasingly more abstract (or schematic) categories that generalize over the similarities of their subtypes. This is illustrated with a simple lexical example in Figure 4a, which shows the relationship between *cat* and *dog* and their taxonomic superordinate *animal*. Analogously, syntagmatically related units give rise to *meronomies*, i.e. part-whole hierarchies in which smaller units are combined into increasingly more complex units. This is depicted in Figure 4b using the example of *the* and *dog*, which compose into *the dog*. The important role of meronomies becomes evident if one considers that phrase-structure diagrams, which are part and parcel of most grammatical analyses, are part-whole hierarchies of increasingly more complex units (Croft 2001). Taxonomic and meronomic hierarchies, and their underlying dimensions of schematicity and complexity, can therefore be regarded as fundamental structuring mechanisms of speakers' grammatical knowledge, which is modeled via "taxonomic and meronymic networks of constructional families" (Barðdal & Gildea 2015: 23).

One question in this context, however, is what types of links constructional networks should incorporate: *vertical links* between units at different hierarchical levels (illustrated by the solid lines in Figure 4), *horizontal links* between units at the same hierarchical level (illustrated by the dashed lines), or both types of links? Specifically, the question is what functions vertical and horizontal links serve in the network, and whether they constitute distinct or potentially overlapping mechanisms. This has been primarily discussed in the context of paradigmatic relations, but the vertical/horizontal distinction can in principle also be applied to syntagmatic relations (see Budts & Petré 2020: 320–321; Langacker 1987: 94–96). In discussions of paradigmatic relations, vertical and horizontal links are often assumed to play fundamentally distinct roles. Vertical links, which were introduced to constructionist theorizing by Lakoff (1987) and Goldberg (1995), are typically couched in terms of *inheritance*, based on the notion that subtypes "inherit," that is, adopt, the features of their supertype (also known as a "schema"; see Daelemans, De Smedt, & Gazdar 1992 for the origins of the concept of "inheritance" in the computational literature). Horizontal relations (also called lateral relations), on the other hand, have been a more recent addition to the CxG literature (Audring 2019; Diessel 2015, 2023; Van de Velde 2014; Perek 2015; Smirnova 2021); they are assumed to relate "similar or contrastive constructions, even when these constructions are not (immediately) subsumed under a schema" (Diessel 2019: 200). Horizontal links have been posited, for example, between alternating variants such as the two English verb-particle constructions (e.g. *turn off the TV* vs. *turn the TV off*; Cappelle 2006; see also Colleman 2020; Zehentner 2019) and between members of constructional paradigms, such as different clause types in Dutch (verb-initial, verb-second, and verb-final; Van de Velde 2014; see also Sommerer 2020; Diewald 2020).

It has been pointed out (Hoffmann 2020; Ungerer in press), however, that some of the scenarios that have been analyzed with horizontal links could be equally captured in terms of vertical relations. For example, alternating constructions can be either connected via a horizontal similarity link, or they can be vertically subsumed under a common schema, in analogy to Figure 4 (compare also Cappelle's [2006: 18] analysis, which includes both vertical and horizontal links). Based on this argument, Hoffmann (2020: 150) argues that the two analyses are empirically indistinguishable in these cases. Ungerer (in press) goes a step further and suggests that a horizontal link between constructions is, by definition, conceptually equivalent to a pair of vertical relations to a schema. The difference, he argues, is only notational, in that vertical analyses make the shared content of the subconstructions explicit while it is merely implicit in a horizontal link. From this perspective, constructional networks could contain either vertical or horizontal relations, but the two would be treated as notational variants rather than as distinct cognitive mechanisms.

Other researchers do not share this view and have continued to highlight the differences between vertical and horizontal links. Zehentner (2019: 324), for instance, suggests that horizontal links may represent similarities of varying strengths, while schemas only emerge if the connections are "very strong, systematic and pervasive." In addition, Diessel (2023: 57–75) argues that only horizontal links can capture relations of similarity and contrast both within constructional families and with other neighboring constructions that do not belong to the family. For example, the verb-particle constructions in

(10a)–(10b) form a constructional family, but they also resemble sentences in which an adjective can either follow or precede the object, as in (10c)–(10d); moreover, (10a) is similar to an intransitive construction with a prepositional phrase, as in (10e). Diessel argues that the existence of horizontal relations such as these is supported by psycholinguistic effects such as priming and by the time course of language acquisition, but that there is no evidence that speakers store a separate schema for each group of similar constructions. In contrast to this position, Ungerer (2022, in press) suggests that priming effects can be equally interpreted as evidence for horizontal links and vertically related schemas, especially if it is assumed that both links and schemas can vary in "strength," that is, in their degree of entrenchment (Hilpert 2015; Langacker 2017; Schmid 2020).

(10)   a. He took off the label.
        b. He took the label off.
        c. He held the door open.
        d. He held open the door.
        e. He jumped off the wall.
        (all from Diessel 2023: 68)

Moving beyond vertical and horizontal relations, researchers have also suggested a number of other linking mechanisms that could be included in constructional networks, besides the "standard" triad of symbolic, paradigmatic, and syntagmatic relations. Goldberg (1995: 74–81), for example, proposed an influential four-way classification of network relations into instance links, subpart links, polysemy links, and metaphorical extension links.[11] The former two largely correspond to paradigmatic and syntagmatic links, with instance links describing relations between subtypes and their paradigmatic supertypes, and subpart links capturing relations between wholes and their parts. Polysemy and metaphorical links, meanwhile, capture specific types of similarities between linguistic units. *Polysemy links* have been posited between the multiple subsenses of constructions such as the ditransitive, which can not only denote "successful transfer of possession" but also "intended transfer," "enabled transfer," and other related meanings (Goldberg 1995: 75–77; see also Croft 2003). *Metaphorical links* have been used, for instance, to relate the literal "change of location" meaning of the caused motion construction to its metaphorical extension as "change of state" in the resultative construction (Goldberg 1995: 81–89).

---

[11] Goldberg (1995) characterizes all four linking types in her model as "inheritance links." Strictly speaking, however, only instance links correspond to the original conception of inheritance as a supertype–subtype relation, while the other three relations constitute distinct mechanisms of information exchange.

Given that both of these links rely on similarity, they could be regarded as special types of paradigmatic relations. Smirnova and Sommerer (2020: 25), for example, reinterpret Goldberg's metaphorical links as a kind of (paradigmatic) horizontal link.[12]

Diessel (2019, 2023) proposes another type of network link, so-called *filler–slot relations* that connect the open slots of constructional schemas to their lexical or phrasal fillers. Filler–slot relations not only capture general facts about the distribution of lexical categories, such as the occurrence of adjectives in attributive position (DET ___ N) or predicative position (NP *be* ___; Diessel 2019: 21), but they also govern the way in which specific lexical items preferentially combine with certain constructions (e.g. the fact that *give* occurs more frequently in the ditransitive than in the *to*-dative; Gries & Stefanowitsch 2004). While filler-slot relations are a useful descriptive tool in these contexts, the question remains of whether they can be ultimately broken down into a combination of paradigmatic and syntagmatic relations. Specifically, the filler seems to stand in a paradigmatic relation with the open slot that it occupies, and this slot is in turn syntagmatically linked to the rest of the abstract construction.

Finally, Schmid (2017a; 2020), working within a related usage-based framework, proposes *pragmatic relations* (or "associations," in his terminology) as a fourth type of network link besides symbolic, paradigmatic, and syntagmatic relations. These pragmatic relations are assumed to connect linguistic items with their context-dependent meanings, including reference, deixis, implicature, and speech acts. Schmid (2020: 48) acknowledges that pragmatic relations are thus similar to symbolic relations but distinguishes the context-dependent mappings of the former from the more system-internal function of the latter. While this view has the advantage of highlighting contextual factors that are otherwise often backgrounded in constructionist network analyses, it faces the well-known difficulty of delimiting the boundary between semantics and pragmatics, or context-independent and context-dependent meaning (Langacker 1987: 154; but see Cappelle 2017 and Leclercq 2020 for discussions of how the distinction can be maintained in CxG).

---

[12] One way in which polysemy and metaphorical links may be different from other paradigmatic links is that they both imply a certain asymmetry. In Goldberg's (1995) conception, polysemy links relate the central prototype of a construction to its sense extensions, while metaphorical links capture the asymmetry between a metaphorical source and a target. This raises its own questions, for example whether these relations are vertical relations (as suggested by Goldberg's analysis in terms of "inheritance") or horizontal (as argued for metaphorical links by Smirnova & Sommerer [2020: 25]), also considering that there are relevant differences between organization by prototypes and taxonomic organization (see Langacker 1987: 380–381).

4.3 Areas for Further Research

As the preceding comments have shown, the architecture of constructional networks, and in particular the types of links included in the model, continue to be a topic of lively discussion among Construction Grammarians. Beyond that, recent work has given rise to a number of other theoretical and empirical questions that are likely to remain on the research agenda for the coming years. We will outline four such research problems in the following, which concern: (i) the relationship between the network nodes and links; (ii) the empirical basis for the representations; (iii) the use of formal and computational tools for network construction and analysis; and (iv) potential limitations of the network model as well as possible alternatives.

Starting with the first point, scholars continue to debate central aspects of the network architecture, among them the question of what the ontological status of the nodes and links is, and what respective roles they play in encoding speakers' linguistic knowledge. Recent work (Hilpert 2018; Hilpert & Diessel 2017; Smirnova & Sommerer 2020) has distinguished between "node-centered" views, which assume that the bulk of the information contained in the network is stored within its nodes, and "connection-centered" views, which assume that speakers' grammatical knowledge resides mainly in the linking patterns between nodes rather than within the nodes themselves. As Hilpert (2018) argues, the connection-centered view lends itself particularly to investigating gradual diachronic developments: For example, the extension of *may* from its deontic to an epistemic meaning can be modeled as a shift in linking patterns between the modal auxiliary and the verbs that it typically combines with (Hilpert 2016; see also Torrent 2015 and Hoffmann & Trousdale 2022 for related approaches). Hilpert (2018: 32–34) argues that the connection-centered view not only captures better the dynamicity of constructional networks over time, but that it is also more compatible with neurophysiological models and computational implementations such as artificial neural networks (see e.g. Pulvermüller 2010 for an approach that combines the latter two).

A radical version of the connection-centered view is presented by Schmid (2017a: 25), who altogether "rejects the distinction between constructions serving as nodes in the network and relations between nodes and instead assumes that linguistic knowledge is available in one format only, namely, associations." One challenge for this perspective, however, is that a network model, by its nature, needs to contain both nodes and links – in other words, there cannot be a "network without nodes." As a result, researchers need to make explicit what kind of information the nodes in their respective models represent. A second relevant issue is Hilpert's (2018: 33) observation that node-centered and connection-centered views are often compatible, and that one can potentially be reformulated in terms of the other (see also the discussion of schemas and horizontal links in Section 4.2). For example, if an abstract construction comes to combine with a new class of lexical fillers, this could either be modeled as a modification of the constructional node itself (e.g. an extension of its meaning pole) or as a change in the links between network units. This is especially true if construction nodes are allowed to be internally complex or "nested," consisting themselves of patterns of interlinked nodes, as we suggested in Section 4.1.

In light of these comments, the relationship between nodes and links in the network may be yet more complex than can be captured with the distinction between node-centered and connection-centered approaches. One possibility is that researchers' choice of what they encode in the nodes and links, respectively, is not primarily determined by some objective reality of what speakers' constructional networks "are like," but rather by pragmatic considerations of which representation best fulfills the purposes of a specific analysis. While an analysis of macro-changes within a constructional family may benefit from a model in which each family member is represented as a single constructional node, an alternative account that zooms into more fine-grained semantic changes may represent the same constructions as clusters of multiple lower-level units. Nevertheless, theoretical arguments and neuropsychological evidence may also place constraints on the plausibility and empirical robustness of certain types of network representations. A major task for future research is therefore to identify criteria and, if possible, quantifiable measures that can be used to determine and compare the descriptive and explanatory adequacy of different network models.

The latter point leads naturally to the second area of ongoing research mentioned at the beginning of this section: the use of empirical data for constructing and testing models of constructional networks. As has frequently been noted (e.g. Croft 2001: 57; Diessel 2019: 16; Tomasello 2003: 98), the question of which network structures speakers plausibly entertain is an empirical one. In particular, this applies to the level of abstraction at which speakers form constructional generalizations, which crucially determines the types of network nodes that researchers posit and the level of granularity at which they conduct their analyses. Traditionally, scholars have largely relied on theoretical argumentation to motivate the existence of constructions at a certain degree of abstraction. In particular, researchers have increasingly posited lower-level schemas at intermediate levels of abstraction rather than highly abstract constructions (e.g. Boas 2003; Dąbrowska 2008; Hartmann 2019; Hilpert 2015). Recently, attempts have also been made to base such modeling decisions on quantifiable factors: Schmid (2020: 234), for example, suggests that the likelihood of speakers forming a schematic construction depends on the frequency and similarity of its instances, as well as the (syntagmatic) size of the pattern and its paradigmatic range.

Frequency can be relatively easily quantified using a variety of well-established corpus measures (Divjak 2019; Gries 2008). Similarity, meanwhile, is more difficult to measure, but relevant evidence could come from a number of corpus-based and experimental methods. On the corpus side, collostructional analysis (see Section 3.3) has been used to compare the typical lexemes that combine with two constructions and thus obtain at least a rough impression of their similarity (Gries 2011; Hartmann 2019). In addition, distributional semantic methods such as semantic vector space analysis (see Lenci 2018 for an overview) yield quantitative measures of the semantic similarity between lexemes – or, if averaging over those lexemes, of the abstract constructions in which they occur – based on their collocational profiles (Hilpert & Perek 2022; Percillier 2020). On the experimental side, priming effects, in particular, are regarded as an important indicator of constructional similarity (Perek 2015; Ungerer 2021, 2022), given that priming tends to be stronger the more similar prime and target are (Branigan & Pickering 2017; see also Section 4.1).

Even with these methods at their disposal, researchers are still several steps away from constructing network representations in a fully bottom-up data-driven way. One challenge is to account for how the different factors, such as frequency and similarity, interact in order to determine the level of abstraction at which constructions are represented. Hilpert (2015, 2021) has begun to sketch out a tentative model of such interactive processes. Using the example of English noun-participle constructions, such as [N-*based*] (e.g. in *computer-based*), the author examines whether an abstract schema that subsumes different noun-participle patterns (e.g. [N-*based*] and [N-*oriented*]) has become more entrenched over the last two centuries (or in Hilpert's words, how much "upward strengthening" the schema has received). The results suggest that some individual noun-participle constructions have become a lot more frequent, but that there has not been the emergence of many new infrequent and semantically dissimilar subtypes that one would expect if the overall schema became more productive. Nevertheless, even though Hilpert's model illustrates important principles of schema formation and potential tools for investigating them, it still lacks a precise formalization and an explicit algorithm for determining degrees of entrenchment among a variety of construction. Further research will thus need to explore whether a clustering algorithm can be constructed that generates constructional categories in a (largely) automatized bottom-up way, based on the frequency and pairwise similarity of their instances.

The latter point again raises another question, addressed here as a third research problem, namely how formal and computational methods can be used to assist the construction and analysis of constructional networks. In particular, the question is to what extent constructionist research can benefit from advances in two areas: first, the use of artificial neural networks (ANNs) to model the emergence of networks and their changes over time; and second, the use of "network science" tools for the analysis of large-scale connectivity patterns.

Starting with ANNs, these methods have had considerable success in modeling, for example, the acquisition of English past-tense morphology (Rumelhart & McClelland 1986) and the lexical categories of nouns and verbs (Elman 1990); more recent applications have targeted the emergence of recursive syntactic structures (Christiansen & MacDonald 2009) and syntactic dependencies (Manning et al. 2020). Importantly, the connectionist architecture of these networks does not map directly onto the symbolic structures that are, at least tacitly, assumed in many constructionist network models (but see e.g. Goldberg [2019: 21], who provides both a symbolic and a distributed example of linguistic representations). Nevertheless, ANNs may still constrain the way in which symbolic networks are constructed, for example by providing estimates of the connection strength between patterns that can then be represented with a symbolic architecture. This is illustrated by Budts and Petré's (2020) study, which provides one example of the still rare application of ANNs in (Diachronic) CxG. Training their model on corpus data between 1580 and 1700, the authors simulate how the distributional profile of periphrastic *do* became increasingly similar to those of modal auxiliaries like *will*, *can*, and *may*. Based on these results, Budts and Petré characterize the development of *do* into an auxiliary during the Early Modern English period as a reconfiguration of its paradigmatic links with similar constructions (see Section 4.2). In line with this example, the role of connectionist networks as a fruitful method for CxG has been recognized (see e.g. Hilpert & Diessel 2017: 71), but their wider application to different areas of constructionist research is still outstanding.

Concerning the second strand of formal methods, "network science" has developed as an interdisciplinary field that uses the mathematical tools of graph theory to describe networks across biology, economics, and the social sciences, among other areas (Barabási 2016; Buchanan 2002). In linguistics, these methods have been used to study different types of networks, including lexical networks (Steyvers & Tenenbaum 2005), phonological networks (Vitevitch 2008), orthographic networks (Siew 2018), networks of linear word co-occurrences (Ferrer i Cancho & Solé 2001), and networks of syntactic dependencies (Ferrer i Cancho, Solé, & Köhler, 2004). While this is not their only application, network science tools are often used to characterize the macrostructure of larger networks and uncover underlying properties that are not apparent to the naked eye. The above-mentioned studies have, for example, illustrated the "small-world" and "scale-free" properties that linguistic networks share with many other phenomena in the natural world: that is, the fact that nodes are on average connected by relatively few steps and that the networks contain "hub" nodes that connect distant network regions with each other.

As with connectionist methods, network science tools have so far been only sparsely applied in constructionist analyses. One notable exception is the work of Ellis, Römer, and O'Donnell (2016), who analyze semantic networks of verbs that occur in prepositional verb constructions such as [V *about* N]. The researchers use the WordNet database (Fellbaum 1998) to construct networks of similarity links among these verbs. They then employ formal network measures such as betweenness centrality, which indicates how often a given node is passed on the shortest path from any place in the network to any other place, to identify well-connected "hub" nodes. This provides a data-driven strategy for identifying semantically more prototypical verbs – which, as Ellis et al. show, are also more likely to be associated with the constructional frame by partici-pants in a free-association experiment. Following their example, future work could explore in more detail how network science methods can be used to analyze constructional networks, especially if larger networks are constructed that are no longer amenable to visual inspection.

As a fourth and final topic, while the last decades of constructionist research have illustrated the descriptive power and cognitive plausibility of construc-tional networks, it is also worth considering what the limitations of the network model are, and what alternative representations may be available. Some poten-tial limitations of the network model have already been mentioned: For example, it requires researchers to distinguish between nodes and links, thus "imposing" a discrete structure on what might ultimately only be continuous patterns of neural activation (see Schmid 2017a). Moreover, current analyses tend to focus on a small number of linking mechanisms in constructional networks, for example the vertical and horizontal relations discussed in Section 4.2 – but the question is whether this two-dimensional structure can do justice to the multidimensional (or, in Goldberg's [2019: 7] terms, "hyperdi-mensional") connections that exist within speakers' linguistic knowledge (see also Smirnova & Sommerer 2020: 31–34; Van Trijp 2020). A related point concerns visualization: Bound by the spatial constraints of traditional print media, the network diagrams used in CxG work usually provide small, simpli-fied illustrations of the theoretical network architecture rather than detailed descriptions of their empirical reality. As such, the diagrams have been criti-cized for providing "static, highly schematized (viz. hierarchical abstraction) and only partial visualizations of the complete grammatical system" (Ibbotson, Salnikov, & Walker 2019: 671). One option for future research may be to combine print publications with external interactive tools, for example as part of electronic supplements, which allow readers to explore more complex constructional networks (and their changes over time) in a suitable virtual interface.

These limitations have also led some researchers to suggest alternative tools for the representation of constructional relations. Fried (2021: 47), for example, proposes a "constructional map" in which constructions – in her study, different types of Czech interactive datives – are not represented as discrete nodes but rather as overlapping shapes within "a contiguous cognitive space." The author suggests that this representation can more adequately capture the partial similarity of constructions that share some of their features but are still difficult to subsume under a taxonomic supertype, as well as the nondiscrete boundaries of the domains (e.g. semantic and interactional) within which the constructions are situated. In contrast to a network in which the number of intervening links, or their weight, expresses the strength of a relation, Fried's constructional map uses the amount of overlap among shapes, as well as their distance in the diagram, to indicate the degree of relatedness between constructions. Naturally, while this kind of representation might exceed the cognitive plausibility of a network diagram, it has its own drawbacks, such as a lesser degree of readability and visual parsimony. It thus remains to be seen how feasible it is to replace (or complement) networks with such other forms of representation.

4.4 Summary

In this section, we have discussed how relations between constructions can be captured in terms of constructional networks. This is a key topic for current constructionist approaches for several reasons. First, a cognitively plausible characterization of linguistic knowledge requires an adequate, and empirically supported, account of how the units that make up a language are organized in the mind. Second, networks provide researchers with a flexible tool to link up the description of synchronic and diachronic phenomena with their underlying psychological mechanisms (e.g. categorization and spreading activation). Third, lexicographic approaches such as the various ongoing "construct-i-con" projects (Lyngfelt et al. 2018; see Section 3.3), which in turn can prove relevant for applied-linguistic contexts such as L2 learning and teaching, often rely on network approaches to characterize the relations between the units they describe.

However, our overview has also highlighted a number of open questions about how exactly constructional networks can or should be modeled. These aspects concern the different types of links that form part of the network structure, but also questions about the empirical foundations of the representations and the methods used to investigate them. Nevertheless, we would argue that the recent attempts to question the theoretical assumptions and practical implementations of the network model should be seen as an encouraging trend. As such, they illustrate the lively role that constructional networks are likely to play within constructionist research in the coming years.

5 Creativity, Multimodality, Individual Differences: Recent Developments in Construction Grammar

Like all scientific paradigms, constructionist approaches have undergone continuous development and tend to follow certain trends and "fashions" over time. In some cases, such trends are closely connected to the overall evolution of a paradigm, as they may emerge from the realization that some important aspects have previously been neglected. This is arguably the case when it comes to the three examples of current developments in CxG that we would like to discuss in this section. Specifically, we will first address constructionist research on linguistic creativity, then turn to multimodality, and finally take a closer look at individual differences among speakers. All these developments are, in a way, a reaction to the emphasis of "mainstream" CxG on more or less "regular" constructional patterns in spoken and written language as well as the tendency to abstract away from the individual language user.

5.1 Linguistic Creativity

Concerning the first aspect, linguistic creativity, Bergs (2018, 2019) points out that the term can refer to two rather different things. On the one hand, in contexts such as child language acquisition, researchers discuss the phenomenon of children starting to use a specific construction creatively (e.g. Tomasello 2003: 107). In this sense, *creative* is more or less synonymous to *productive*. Children – and also adults – extend an existing rule to new cases, without, however, "bending" the rules. On the other hand, the term creativity also refers to cases in which language users go beyond the rules. Bauer (2001: 64), for example, defines creativity as "the extension of non-productive patterns" (see Barðdal [2008: 3] for discussion). To distinguish between these two meanings, Sampson (2016: 19) suggests the term *F-creativity* (for "fixed creativity"), referring to "activities which characteristically produce examples drawn from a fixed and known (. . .) range," and *E-creativity* (for "enlarging" or "extending creativity"), which refers to "activities which characteristically produce examples that enlarge our understanding of the range of possible products of the activity."

Bergs (2018) identifies three different sources for E-creativity in language: (i) performance errors, such as slips of the tongue; (ii) language contact, for instance through borrowing; and (iii) the intentional manipulation of linguistic material. The latter type of E-creativity, in particular, can be connected to the notion of linguistic *extravagance*, which refers to speakers' desire to talk in such a way that they are noticed (Haspelmath 1999; Keller 1994; Ungerer & Hartmann 2020). One example of this is "snowcloning," that is, the use of formulaic patterns that usually draw on a more-or-less-fixed template (Hartmann & Ungerer 2023; Traugott & Trousdale 2013: 183–186). Frequently mentioned examples of snowclones include [*the mother of all* X], as in *Hoffmann (2022) is the mother of all Construction Grammar textbooks*, or [X *BE the new* Y], as in *Ungerer and Hartmann are the new Ungerer and Schmid*. Snowclones are interesting from a constructionist perspective for at least two reasons. First, they are prime examples of partially fixed constructions, as they consist of a lexically fixed part and one or more open slots. Second, they fulfill specific pragmatic and interpersonal functions: On the one hand, they typically display extravagant characteristics, such as the hyperbolic meaning of *the mother of all X* or the quasi-paradoxical comparisons inherent in many instances of *X is the new Y* (e.g. *small is the new big*). On the other hand, snowclones also adhere to what Haspelmath (1999) calls the maxim of conformity, that is, the desire to talk like others talk (Keller 1994). As such, snowclones illustrate the interplay between the two opposing maxims of extravagance and conformity, functioning both as creative patterns while also being instantly recognizable by members of the (frequently online) communities in which they are propagated.

As with many concepts that are part and parcel of constructionist approaches, we cannot draw a clear line between E-creativity and F-creativity, as they blend into one another. A construction that emerges as an E-creative pattern can become an inconspicuous, run-of-the-mill construction if it is used often enough. A classic example are the developments described by Jespersen's cycle (Jespersen 1917; Mosegaard Hansen 2011): An item that is originally used to emphasize negation, such as French *pas* (originally 'step'), becomes a part of the negation pattern (French *ne . . . pas*). This is also true for the creative use of words: The German word *Kopf* 'head,' for example, is cognate to English *cup*, which is also what it originally denoted. The human head was metaphorically, and probably jokingly, referred to as a vessel. The original semantics of the term is not transparent anymore to present-day language users, however, and *Kopf* has become the unmarked default term for "head."

These examples illustrate a number of challenges that constructionist approaches face when dealing with creativity. First, social-pragmatic dimensions of constructional knowledge have to be taken into account. Most constructionist approaches are aware of the importance of this dimension, but only few operationalize it in a systematic way. Schmid (2020), for instance, while not explicitly working in a constructionist framework, posits pragmatic associations to account for such phenomena within his entrenchment-and-conventionalization model (see also Section 4.2). Second, these socio-pragmatic features are a moving target, illustrating once again the dynamics of linguistic signs and constructions. Like other aspects of meaning, socio-pragmatic aspects of constructions can bleach, and as an initially infrequent construction is used more regularly, it can lose its salience. One concept that aims at capturing this continuum is Barðdal's (2008) productivity cline, which ranges from analogical extension to full productivity. For instance, early uses of the suffix[13] *-gate* 'scandal,' as in *Koreagate* (a 1976 bribery scandal),[14] can be seen as analogical coinages based on *Watergate*. As the suffix became more and more productive, it is possible that it has gradually lost the connection to its source and that more recent formations like *Partygate* (referring to the prime minister of a peculiar island country celebrating parties during Covid lockdowns) are not coined in analogy to *Watergate* anymore but rather make use of a schema [X-*gate*] that is now independent from its source.

Third, Hoffmann (2018: 271–272) mentions the importance of taking individual differences in the use of creative language into account, citing psychological research that shows a strong correlation between creativity and personality traits like openness and extroversion. A crucial question that follows from this perspective is *why* and *by whom* creative constructions are coined, and how they spread in the language community. This is also connected to some of the key questions in historical linguistics: Who are the agents of language change, and how do linguistic innovations emerge and spread? Research on linguistic creativity and individual differences (see Section 5.3) can arguably help provide answers to such questions.

5.2 Multimodality and Signed Languages

Importantly, mechanisms of creativity and dynamic change are of course not limited to the spoken modality. Recent research has also focused on signed languages on the one hand, and on co-speech gesture on the other. While both make use of the manual-visual modality, it is important to note that sign languages are fully-fledged languages in their own right, while co-speech

---

[13] The morphological status of *-gate* is subject to debate (see Flach, Kopf, & Stefanowitsch 2018: 246–247), but there is an emerging consensus that it can be seen as a combining form. Flach et al. (2018) use the alternative term *confix* for this, while Norde and Sippach (2019) adopt a term proposed by Arnold Zwicky in a blog post and call such "liberated" parts of words *libfixes*.

[14] See https://en.wikipedia.org/wiki/Koreagate (last checked 22/10/2022).

gesture accompanies spoken language. Following Kendon (e.g. 2004: 99–106) and McNeill (2016: 5), we can posit a continuum from gesticulation via pantomime to sign language, with gesture accompanying speech, while signs in signed languages are "*not* accompanied by speech [...], and the languages themselves have the essential properties of all languages" (McNeill 2011: 344, emphasis original).

Lepic and Occhino (2018: 143–146) observe that the field of sign language linguistics has left a few potentially fallacious assumptions of structuralist theory unquestioned, including the division of linguistic knowledge into two types, "lexicon" and "grammar," and propose that a constructionist analysis could help overcome a number of problems that arise from these assumptions. For example, a strict lexicon/grammar division requires linguistic units to be assigned to one of those categories, even though there is good evidence that even fully transparent structures may be cognitively entrenched (see Section 2.2) – Langacker (1987: 42) calls this the rule/list fallacy. In the area of sign language linguistics, this is relevant for the question of which signs are considered to be part of the mental lexicon. Lepic and Occhino (2018: 148) show that traditionally, "unanalyzed" signs have been treated as listed in the lexicon – however, this is problematic, as "signers readily 'reanalyze' the structure of 'unanalyzed' signs in the course of normal signing." A constructionist approach allows researchers not only to characterize the internal structure of signs as continuous rather than discrete but also to arrange them along a gradient cline from gesture to language in the spirit of Kendon's and McNeill's gesture continuum (Lepic & Occhino 2018: 162–167). This also makes it possible to use similar analytical tools for the investigation of signed languages on the one hand, and co-speech gesture on the other.

As for the latter, another key discussion within CxG revolves around the assumption of multimodal constructions: It is a matter of debate to what extent co-speech gestures can be conceived of as an integral part of constructions. For example, Zima (2014) argues that constructions like [V_{motion} *in circles*] (e.g. *we ended up going in circles for twenty minutes*) and [*all the way from* X PREP Y] (e.g. *all the way from the Seattle area down through Oregon*) are accompanied by specific gestures so frequently and systematically that it makes sense to speak of multimodal constructions. As usage-based constructionist approaches assume that linguistic knowledge is rooted in embodied experience (Lakoff 1987), it stands to reason to assume that this experience is not limited to strictly linguistic features but encompasses paralinguistic features like prosody, pitch, and intonation as well as features traditionally seen as nonlinguistic, such as gesture (see e.g. Cienki 2013, 2017; Lanwer 2017).

Feyaerts, Brône, and Oben (2017) and Schoonjans (2017), however, point to an important issue in this context: Most authors arguing for multimodal constructions "stress the systematicity of the multimodal co-occurrences in corpus data as an argument for their construction status" (Feyaerts et al. 2017: 147). Yet as we have seen above, the frequency criterion is a complex issue for CxG in general, and given that there is usually more room for individual variation in the domain of multimodal constructions than in the case of linguistic signs, it is even harder to determine when the co-occurrence of verbal and gestural patterns can count as a construction. In principle, arguments similar to the ones that have been brought forward against the frequency criterion in the definition of constructions (see Section 2.2) can be used to argue against the assumption of multimodal constructions. One key aspect that has to be taken into account is that the nonverbal elements that form part of putative multimodal constructions are rarely, if ever, obligatory. Ziem (2017), for example, argues that there is no clear evidence for the existence of *inherently* multimodal constructions, that is, constructions in which the nonverbal elements form an integral part of the construction's form side. Then again, if we take the idea seriously that language is a highly dynamic system and that our knowledge of constructions is vast and redundant, rather than limited and highly economic, it does make sense to assume that knowledge about typically co-occurring co-speech gestures or other nonverbal elements can form part of a language user's knowledge of a construction. As such, many of the open questions regarding Multimodal CxG hark back to overarching questions of constructionist approaches (see Schoonjans 2017), including the crucial question of how the key notion of construction is defined and operationalized.

Another example of multimodality concerns the interaction of text and images, for example in Internet memes (Bülow, Merten, & Johann, 2018; Dancygier & Vandelanotte 2017). A subtype of these, so-called image-macro memes, consist of a more-or-less fixed image and a text that can display different degrees of variability. For example, in the case of the Merkel–Obama meme studied by Bülow et al. (2018), the image shows Angela Merkel spreading her arms in front of Barack Obama, who is sitting on a bench. This gesture can be interpreted quite differently, as suggested by the captions, which vary from *Give Mommy a big hug*, referencing an embracing gesture, to *Wir sagen 2-Grad-Ziel und tun nichts. Who cares?* 'We say 2-degree goal and do nothing. Who cares?,' which indexes an exaggerated shrug gesture signaling indifference. Bülow et al. (2018) also find that many of the captions contain the pattern *soooo* combined with an adjective, for example *Echt jetzt? Das Internet gibt es schon soooo lange?* 'Really? The Internet has already existed for soooo long?,' which alludes to Merkel's much-ridiculed statement (during a press conference with Obama in

2013) that the Internet was still *Neuland* 'new territory' for everyone. This example also shows that Internet memes tap into rich encyclopedic background knowledge. The same is true for the *One does not simply* meme investigated by Dancygier and Vandelanotte (2017), which contains a screenshot from the film *The Lord of the Rings: The Fellowship of the Ring*, accompanied by a variation of the film quote *One does not simply walk into Mordor*. One of the examples the authors discuss is *One does not simply save Africa by donating $1*, which evokes cultural knowledge about donation campaigns in addition to the background knowledge about the film that is required to process the meme. Moreover, by reproducing a lexically fixed part of the original (*One does not simply . . .*), this type of meme shows resemblance to the "snowclones" discussed in Section 5.1 and could thus be seen as a multimodal extension of the latter (see Hartmann & Ungerer 2023).

The reason for treating Internet memes as constructions is that they can be considered partially schematic pairings of form and function. The image in particular contributes aspects of conventionalized meaning that cannot be compositionally derived from the caption text. For instance, the *Scumbag Steve* meme also discussed by Dancygier and Vandelanotte (2017) imposes a specific viewpoint, characterizing the action or stance expressed in the caption text as socially inappropriate (e.g. *Breaks something expensive of yours – "Why would you spend that much on it anyway?"*). While Dancygier and Vandelanotte (2017: 591–592) concede that an analysis as constructions may not be appropriate for all meme types, such as spoof videos (parody videos), they do argue that image-macro memes can be regarded as multimodal constructions. Moreover, they suggest that "Just as construction grammar has long recognized clines of constructionality in dimensions of size [. . .] and abstractness [. . .], we might begin to conceive of gradations in terms of modalities involved (from monomodal to multimodal)" (Dancygier & Vandelanotte 2017: 591).

Finally, another modality that has not yet been explored in detail from a constructionist perspective but that would merit further investigation is written language. Within the emerging field of grapholinguistics (Meletis 2020; Meletis & Dürscheid 2022; Neef 2015), written language is regarded as more than just a representation of spoken language, but rather a modality to be studied in its own right. For one thing, writing affords a number of resources that are unique to this modality, such as capitalization and punctuation. For another, there is psycho- and neurolinguistic evidence that the processes of reading and writing may not function with recourse to speech (see e.g. Dehaene 2009; Meletis & Dürscheid 2022: 28–29). From a constructionist point of view, this means that, at the very least, graphemic properties should be taken into consideration when describing the form side of constructions (Geyer, Bick, & Kleene 2022: 247). But going a step further, the question is whether the standard inventory of constructions should be complemented by graphemic constructions, especially if we adopt a broad notion of constructionhood like the one we have applied to image-macro memes. Consider, for instance, the expressive use of multiple exclamation marks <!!!> (see e.g. Busch 2021: 326), or the use of sentence-internal capital letters in German, whose main role in present-day language can be considered metalinguistic (viz., marking heads of noun phrases). These graphic devices fulfill functions that do not have a direct counterpart in other modalities. If we adopt a broad concept of constructions in the sense of mentally internalized generalizations that also allows for the possibility of, for instance, gestural constructions, then it does not seem too far-fetched to allow for graphemic constructions as well. At the same time, however, as we have seen, it is an open question whether such an extension of the construction concept is desirable, or whether a narrower notion of constructions will prove more useful for linguistic analysis.

In sum, these examples show that language users make use of a wide range of semiotic resources, both linguistic and paralinguistic as well as nonlinguistic. Constructionist approaches are arguably well equipped to explore all these facets of communication, as most of their key concepts are neither tied to a specific modality nor strictly limited to linguistic signs. In many respects, however, multimodal CxG is still in its infancy, and a constructionist approach to grapholinguistics has yet to be developed.

5.3 Individual Differences

The overarching questions regarding the definition and operationalization of constructions are closely connected to the last of the three aspects to be discussed in this section: If we conceive of CxG as a theory of linguistic knowledge, the question arises of *whose* linguistic knowledge it is that we are actually describing. The fact that Construction Grammarians for a long time tended to abstract away from individual differences might be a bit surprising at first glance, as the declared goal of the paradigm is "to find out what speakers know when they know a language and to describe this knowledge as accurately as possible" (Hilpert 2013: 1–2). From this perspective, it is crucial to take the level of the individual into account, especially given the mounting evidence that speakers differ significantly in their linguistic knowledge (e.g. Dąbrowska 2012). In recent years, this perspective has become ever more important in constructionist approaches, and in usage-based linguistics in general (see e.g. Petré & Anthonissen 2020). Nevertheless, much work in constructionist frameworks can be criticized for paying lip service to this commitment while at the same time retaining, at least implicitly, the concept of an "ideal speaker-hearer" (Chomsky 1965). The latter assumption is also intertwined with potentially problematic notions such as that of a standard language, which in turn is often tied to language ideologies (see e.g. Walsh 2021).

A perspective that emphasizes individual differences follows straightforwardly from a usage-based account: If language is learned through experience, as argued by the usage-based approach to language acquisition (e.g. Tomasello 2003; Tomasello & Lieven 2008), each person will build up their own "construct-i-con" as every individual encounters at least somewhat different linguistic input. What makes matters even more complex is that a person's construct-i-con can change over the course of a lifetime (see e.g. Neels 2020). Charting intra- and interindividual differences is a challenge for research on language acquisition, language variation, and language change. But constructionist approaches are arguably well suited to meet this challenge as they, at least in principle, offer the possibility of modeling individual-specific constructional networks. While there are still some open questions about how exactly this could be done, the recent surge in research on individual differences promises significant progress regarding the development of analytical tools for addressing these issues (see e.g. Anthonissen & Petré 2019; Beaman & Buchstaller 2021; Schmid & Mantlik 2015; Standing & Petré 2021). The turn toward individual differences is also a consequence of the commitment of usage-based approaches to putting actual language use center stage.

As one example of a study investigating individual differences, consider Neels' (2020) analysis of the *let alone* construction in the works of William Faulkner. Comparing Faulkner's novels with the Fiction part of the Corpus of Historical American English (COHA), Neels shows that Faulkner was way ahead of his contemporaries in the use of this construction, using it more and more over his lifespan, and increasingly varying the constituent types in the X and Y slot of [X, *let alone* Y] as well as the syntactic positioning of *let alone*. To some extent, then, the development of the construction in Faulkner's idiolect can be regarded as anticipating the community-wide grammaticalization of the construction. In a similar vein, Schmid and Mantlik (2015) investigate the construction [N *BE that*], such as *all the talk is that* . . ., in the language use of eighteenth- and nineteenth-century authors, showing that their usage profiles differed in terms of the frequency with which they used the construction as well as the construction's collocational range. These differences turn out to be much larger than expected even for authors whose works can be considered very similar in terms of parameters like genre and style (Schmid & Mantlik 2015: 616). Especially from a diachronic point of view, then, processes at the micro-level of individuals can prove highly informative, as they allow us to bridge the gap between entrenchment, as a process that primarily takes place at the level of the individual, and conventionalization, as a process that unfolds at the level of the community (see e.g. Schmid 2020).

5.4 Summary

Summing up, constructionist approaches are currently extending their scope, taking numerous aspects into account that may have been implicit in the assumptions of the paradigm but which arguably remained understudied until fairly recently. We have discussed three examples of topics that are currently gaining traction in constructionist research: the role of creativity, especially in the sense of "rule-breaking" creativity that entails extravagant effects; multi-modal perspectives on language; and individual differences among speakers. More topics could easily be added to this list, including the recent endeavors in "constructicography," that is, attempts to document the constructional inventories of different languages (Herbst 2019; Lyngfelt et al. 2018; see Section 3.3), the related question of how exactly formal and semantic aspects of constructions can be cross-linguistically mapped onto each other in an empirically valid way (see e.g. Willich 2022), the question of how multilingualism can be modeled in a CxG framework (Höder 2012, 2014; Wasserscheidt 2015, 2021), and proposals for how constructionist principles can be applied to language pedagogy (Boas 2022; De Knop & Gilquin 2016). These examples show that constructionist approaches continue to evolve in multiple productive directions, both in terms of theory and those of methodology.

6 Conclusion and Outlook

Surveying the recent CxG literature, one might gain the impression that constructionist approaches are notoriously self-reflexive – compare paper titles like "Three open questions in Diachronic Construction Grammar" (Hilpert 2018) or "What would it take for us to abandon Construction Grammar?" (Hoffmann 2020). The present Element is no exception, as giving an overview of current developments in CxG necessarily requires a discussion of the many different ways in which basic concepts such as that of "construction" have been, and are being, implemented in different streams of constructionist research. But we hope to have shown that the heterogeneity of constructionist approaches can actually be seen as a strength of the paradigm, as it allows for approaching research questions in different, yet often complementary, ways.

One reason why much of the recent work in CxG has taken a metatheoretical perspective is that there are a number of unresolved key questions, some of which we have addressed in this Element. The most important one is probably that of how exactly the notion of construction is defined, and which types of linguistic units it encompasses. In Section 2, we showed that there is a broad consensus that constructions can be conceived of as form–meaning pairs at various levels of abstraction and complexity. However, it is a matter of debate whether morphemes and/or words can be considered as constructions. In line with the recent tendency in usage-based linguistics to conceive of language as a complex adaptive system (Beckner et al. 2009), we have argued for a dynamic and gradient notion of constructionhood. Another question is whether the number of different constructionist approaches, and their theoretical and methodological divergences, strengthen the paradigm or whether they lead to a fragmentation of the field. In Section 3, we reviewed six major constructionist frameworks, arguing that they pursue somewhat different but mutually complementary research goals, and that their analyses often require different methods and degrees of formalization. A third issue, which we addressed in Section 4, concerns the dynamic nature of language and how it can be modeled via different types of network relations between constructions. We discussed the potential and challenges of current network models in CxG, addressing aspects such as the ontological status of the network units, the empirical basis for network representations, and the use of formal tools like those of network science for the analysis of connectivity patterns.

Finally, in Section 5, we introduced three topics that have recently become more important in constructionist research: linguistic creativity, multimodality, and individual differences. While these examples show that CxG is extending its scope, taking phenomena into account that had previously been neglected, there are still a number of desiderata. One is extending constructionist approaches to a broader inventory of different languages. While there has been much progress regarding the adaptation of constructionist analyses to a more diverse set of languages, including ones that are understudied (see e.g. Hölzl 2018 for a constructionist account of negation constructions in Manchu), most constructionist theorizing still focuses on a small set of WEIRD languages (in the sense of Henrich, Heine, & Norenzayan 2010, i.e. languages spoken in Western, Educated, Industrialized, Rich, and Democratic societies). This problem is not limited to constructionist approaches, but it is particularly relevant for CxG as it is still to some extent an open question how well constructionist concepts can account for typologically very different languages, including signed languages, as discussed in Section 5.2. Another challenge concerns the cognitive plausibility of constructions and relations between constructions. While there have been many attempts to bring together empirical evidence using multiple different methods (see e.g. Schönefeld 2011), these are often limited to individual case studies that can lead to very different conclusions when individual researchers try to derive bigger-picture conclusions from them. Such differences can either give rise to a fragmentation of the field, or to fruitful and productive discussions. We hope that our approach in the present Element will contribute to the latter, by highlighting specific points of divergence and suggesting a number of possible avenues for future research.

Despite the remaining questions and challenges, constructionist approaches have become a major paradigm in the study of language. The concept of constructions offers a unified framework for investigating phenomena at different levels of linguistic analysis and for modeling grammatical knowledge in a way that is gradually becoming more and more cognitively plausible. But even after more than thirty years, the constructionist enterprise has only just begun, and, to close with the obligatory pun, CxG as a field and as a family of theories is still very much under construction.

References

Abbot-Smith, K. & Behrens, H. (2006). How known constructions influence the acquisition of other constructions: The German passive and future constructions. *Cognitive Science*, **30**(6), 995–1026. DOI: https://doi.org/10.1207/s15516709cog0000_61.

Ambridge, B. (2020). Against stored abstractions: A radical exemplar model of language acquisition. *First Language*, **40**(5–6), 509–559. DOI: https://doi.org/10.1177/0142723719869731.

Ambridge, B. & Lieven, E. (2011). *Child Language Acquisition: Contrasting Theoretical Approaches*. Cambridge: Cambridge University Press. DOI: https://doi.org/10.1017/CBO9780511975073.

Anderson, J. R. (1983). A spreading activation theory of memory. *Journal of Verbal Learning & Verbal Behavior*, **22**(3), 261–295. DOI: https://doi.org/10.1016/S0022-5371(83)90201-3.

Anderson, S. E., Matlock, T. & Spivey, M. (2013). Grammatical aspect and temporal distance in motion descriptions. *Frontiers in Psychology*, **4**, article no. 337. DOI: https://doi.org/10.3389/fpsyg.2013.00337.

Anthonissen, L., & Petré, P. (2019). Grammaticalization and the linguistic individual: New avenues in lifespan research. *Linguistics Vanguard*, **5**(s2), article no. 20180037. DOI: https://doi.org/10.1515/lingvan-2018-0037

Audring, J. (2019). Mothers or sisters? The encoding of morphological knowledge. *Word Structure*, **12**(3), 274–296. DOI: https://doi.org/10.3366/word.2019.0150.

Baker, P. & Egbert, J. (eds.). (2016). *Triangulating Methodological Approaches in Corpus-Linguistic Research*. New York: Routledge.

Barabási, A.-L. (2016). *Network Science*. Cambridge: Cambridge University Press.

Barðdal, J. (2008). *Productivity: Evidence from Case and Argument Structure in Icelandic*. Amsterdam: John Benjamins. DOI: https://doi.org/10.1075/cal.8.

Barðdal, J. & Gildea, S. (2015). Diachronic construction grammar: Epistemological context, basic assumptions and historical implications. In J. Barðdal, E. Smirnova, L. Sommerer & S. Gildea (eds.), *Diachronic Construction Grammar*, 1–50. Amsterdam: John Benjamins. DOI: https://doi.org/10.1075/cal.18.01bar.

Barlow, M. & Kemmer, S. (eds.). (2000). *Usage-Based Models of Grammar*. Stanford: CSLI Publications.

Barrès, V. (2017). *Template Construction Grammar: A Schema-Theoretic Computational Construction Grammar*. Papers from the 2017 AAAI Spring Symposia SS-17–02, pp. 139–146.

Barsalou, L. W. (1999). Perceptual symbol systems. *Behavioral and Brain Sciences*, **22**(4), 577–660. DOI: https://doi.org/10.1017/s0140525x 99002149.

Bauer, L. (2001). *Morphological Productivity*. Cambridge: Cambridge University Press. DOI: https://doi.org/10.1017/CBO9780511486210.

Beaman, K. V. & Buchstaller, I. (eds.). (2021). *Language Variation and Language Change Across the Lifespan: Theoretical and Empirical Perspectives from Panel Studies*. New York: Routledge. DOI: https://doi.org/10.4324 /9780429030314.

Beckner, C., Blythe, R., Bybee, J. et al. (2009). Language is a complex adaptive system: Position paper. *Language Learning*, **59** Suppl. 1, 1–26. DOI: https:// doi.org/10.1111/j.1467-9922.2009.00533.x.

Behrens, H. (2021). Constructivist approaches to first language acquisition. *Journal of Child Language*, **48**(5), 959–983. DOI: https://doi.org/10.1017 /S0305000921000556.

Bell, M. J., Ben Hedia, S. & Plag, I. (2021). How morphological structure affects phonetic realisation in English compound nouns. *Morphology*, **31**(2), 87–120. DOI: https://doi.org/10.1007/s11525-020-09346-6.

Bencini, G. M. L. & Goldberg, A. E. (2000). The contribution of argument structure constructions to sentence meaning. *Journal of Memory and Language*, **43**(4), 640–651. DOI: https://doi.org/10.1006/jmla.2000.2757.

Bergen, B. (2007). Experimental methods for simulation semantics. In M. Gonzalez-Marquez, I. Mittelberg, S. Coulson, & M. J. Spivey (eds.), *Methods in Cognitive Linguistics*. Amsterdam: John Benjamins, pp. 277–301. DOI: https://doi.org/10.1075/hcp.18.19ber.

Bergen, B. & Chang, N. (2005). Embodied Construction Grammar in simulation-based language understanding. In J.-O. Östman & M. Fried (eds.), *Construction Grammars: Cognitive Grounding and Theoretical Extensions*. Amsterdam: John Benjamins, pp. 147–190. DOI: https://doi.org/10.1075/cal .3.08ber.

Bergen, B. & Chang, N. (2013). Embodied Construction Grammar. In T. Hoffmann & G. Trousdale (eds.), *The Oxford Handbook of Construction Grammar*. Oxford: Oxford University Press, pp. 168–190. DOI: https://doi .org/10.1093/oxfordhb/9780195396683.013.0010.

Bergs, A. (2010). Expressions of futurity in contemporary English: A Construction Grammar perspective. *English Language & Linguistics*, **14**(2), 217–238. DOI: https://doi.org/10.1017/S1360674310000067.

Bergs, A. (2018). Learn the rules like a pro, so you can break them like an artist (Picasso): Linguistic aberrancy from a constructional perspective. *Zeitschrift für Anglistik und Amerikanistik*, **66**(3), 277–293. DOI: https://doi.org/10 .1515/zaa-2018-0025.

Bergs, A. (2019). What, if anything, is linguistic creativity? *Gestalt Theory*, **41**(2), 173–183. DOI: https://doi.org/10.2478/gth-2019-0017.

Beuls, K. (2017). An open-ended computational construction grammar for Spanish verb conjugation. *Constructions and Frames*, **9**(2), 278–301. DOI: https://doi.org/10.1075/cf.00005.beu.

Blumenthal-Dramé, A. (2012). *Entrenchment in Usage-Based Theories: What Corpus Data Do and Do Not Reveal About the Mind*. Berlin: De Gruyter. DOI: https://doi.org/10.1515/9783110294002.

Boas, H. C. (2003). *A Constructional Approach to Resultatives*. Stanford, CA: CSLI Publications.

Boas, H. C. (2013). Cognitive Construction Grammar. In T. Hoffmann & G. Trousdale (eds.), *The Oxford Handbook of Construction Grammar*. Oxford: Oxford University Press, pp. 233–252. DOI: https://doi.org/10 .1093/oxfordhb/9780195396683.013.0013.

Boas, H. C. (2021). Construction Grammar and frame semantics. In X. Wen & J. R. Taylor (eds.), *The Routledge Handbook of Cognitive Linguistics*, 43–77. New York: Routledge, pp. 43–77. DOI: https://doi.org/10.4324 /9781351034708-5.

Boas, H. C. (ed.). (2022). *Directions for Pedagogical Construction Grammar: Learning and Teaching (with) Constructions*. Berlin: De Gruyter. DOI: https://doi.org/10.1515/9783110746723.

Boas, H. C. & Sag, I. A. (eds.). (2012). *Sign-Based Construction Grammar*. Stanford, CA: CSLI Publications.

Bock, J. K. (1986). Syntactic persistence in language production. *Cognitive Psychology*, **18**(3), 355–387. DOI: https://doi.org/10.1016/0010-0285(86) 90004-6.

Bolinger, D. (1976). Meaning and memory. *Forum Linguisticum*, **1**, 1–14. DOI: https://doi.org/10.1515/9783110815733.95.

Booij, G. (2002). The balance between storage and computation in phonology. In S. Nooteboom, F. Weerman, & F. Wijnen (eds.), *Storage and Computation in the Language Faculty*. Dordrecht: Springer, pp. 133–156. DOI: https://doi .org/10.1007/978-94-010-0355-1_5.

Booij, G (2010). *Construction Morphology*. Oxford: Oxford University Press.

Booij, G. (2012). *The Grammar of Words: An Introduction to Linguistic Morphology*, 3rd ed. Oxford: Oxford University Press.

Booij, G. (2017). Inheritance and motivation in Construction Morphology. In N. Gisborne & A. Hippisley (eds.), *Defaults in Morphological Theory.* Oxford: Oxford University Press, pp. 18–39. DOI: https://doi.org/10.1093 /oso/9780198712329.003.0002.

Branigan, H. P. & Pickering, M. J. (2017). An experimental approach to linguistic representation. *Behavioral and Brain Sciences*, **40**, E282. DOI: https://doi.org/10.1017/S0140525X16002028.

Brenier, J. M. & Michaelis, L. A. (2005). Optimization via syntactic amalgam: Syntax-prosody mismatch and copula doubling. *Corpus Linguistics and Linguistic Theory*, **1**(1), 45–88. DOI: https://doi.org/10.1515/cllt.2005.1.1.45.

Bryant, J. E. (2008). Best-fit constructional analysis. PhD dissertation, University of California, Berkeley.

Buchanan, M. (2002). *Nexus: Small Worlds and the Groundbreaking Science of Networks.* New York: W. W. Norton.

Budts, S. (2022). A connectionist approach to analogy: On the modal meaning of periphrastic DO in Early Modern English. *Corpus Linguistics and Linguistic Theory*, **18**(2), 337–364. DOI: https://doi.org/10.1515/cllt-2019-0080.

Budts, S. & Petré, P. (2020). Putting connections centre stage in diachronic Construction Grammar. In L. Sommerer & E. Smirnova (eds.), *Nodes and Networks in Diachronic Construction Grammar.* Amsterdam: John Benjamins, pp. 317–351. DOI: https://doi.org/10.1075/cal.27.09bud.

Bülow, L., Merten, M.-L. & Johann, M. (2018). Internet-Memes als Zugang zu multimodalen Konstruktionen. *Zeitschrift für Angewandte Linguistik*, **2018** (69), 1–32. DOI: https://doi.org/10.1515/zfal-2018-0015.

Busch, F. (2021). *Digitale Schreibregister: Kontexte, Formen und metaprag-matische Reflexionen.* Berlin: De Gruyter. DOI: https://doi.org/10.1515 /9783110728835.

Busso, L., Perek, F. & Lenci, A. (2021). Constructional associations trump lexical associations in processing valency coercion. *Cognitive Linguistics*, **32** (2), 287–318. DOI: https://doi.org/10.1515/cog-2020-0050.

Bybee, J. (1998). The emergent lexicon. *Chicago Linguistic Society*, **34**, 421–435.

Bybee, J. (2000). The phonology of the lexicon: Evidence from lexical diffu-sion. In M. Barlow & S. Kemmer (eds.), *Usage-Based Models of Language.* Stanford: CSLI Publications, pp. 65–85.

Bybee, J. (2010). *Language, Usage and Cognition.* Cambridge: Cambridge University Press. DOI: https://doi.org/10.1017/CBO9780511750526.

Bybee, J. (2013). Usage-based theory and exemplar representations of construc-tions. In T. Hoffmann & G. Trousdale (eds.), *The Oxford Handbook of*

Construction Grammar. Oxford: Oxford University Press, pp. 49–69. DOI: https://doi.org/10.1093/oxfordhb/9780195396683.013.0004.

Bybee, J. L. & Hopper, P. J. (2001). *Frequency and the Emergence of Linguistic Structure.* Amsterdam: John Benjamins. DOI: https://doi.org/10.1075/tsl.45.

Cappelle, B. (2006). Particle placement and the case for "allostructions." *Constructions,* Special Volume **1,** 1–28. DOI: https://doi.org/10.24338/cons-381.

Cappelle, B. (2017). What's pragmatics doing outside constructions? In I. Depraetere & R. Salkie (eds.), *Semantics and Pragmatics: Drawing a Line.* Cham: Springer, pp. 115–151. DOI: https://doi.org/10.1007/978-3-319-32247-6_8.

Cappelle, B. & Depraetere, I. (eds.). (2016). Modal meaning in Construction Grammar [Special issue]. *Constructions and Frames,* **8**(1). DOI: https://doi.org/10.1075/cf.8.1.

Casenhiser, D. & Goldberg, A. E. (2005). Fast mapping between a phrasal form and meaning. *Developmental Science,* **8**(6), 500–508. https://doi.org/10.1111/j.1467-7687.2005.00441.x.

Cienki, A. (2013). Cognitive linguistics: Spoken language and gesture as expressions of conceptualization. In C. Müller, A. Cienki, E. Fricke et al. (eds.), *Body – Language – Communication: An International Handbook on Multimodality in Human Interaction,* vol. 1. Berlin: De Gruyter, pp. 182–201. DOI: https://doi.org/10.1515/9783110261318.182.

Cienki, A. (2017). Utterance Construction Grammar (UCxG) and the variable multimodality of constructions. *Linguistics Vanguard,* **3**(s1), article no. 20160048. DOI: https://doi.org/10.1515/lingvan-2016-0048.

Chomsky, N. (1965). *Aspects of the Theory of Syntax.* Cambridge, MA: MIT Press.

Chomsky, N. (1981). *Lectures on Government and Binding.* Dordrecht: Foris.

Christensen, P., Fusaroli, R. & Tylén, K. (2016). Environmental constraints shaping constituent order in emerging communication systems: Structural iconicity, interactive alignment and conventionalization. *Cognition,* **146,** 67–80. DOI: https://doi.org/10.1016/j.cognition.2015.09.004.

Christiansen, M. H. & MacDonald, M. C. (2009). A usage-based approach to recursion in sentence processing. *Language Learning,* **59**(s1), 126–161. DOI: https://doi.org/10.1111/j.1467-9922.2009.00538.x.

Colleman, T. (2020). The emergence of the dative alternation in Dutch: Towards the establishment of a horizontal link. In C. Fedriani & M. Napoli (eds.), *The*

Diachrony of Ditransitives. Berlin: De Gruyter, pp. 137–168. DOI: https://doi.org/10.1515/9783110701371-005.

Colleman, T. & Noël, D. (2012). The Dutch evidential NCI: A case of constructional attrition. *Journal of Historical Pragmatics*, **13**(1), 1–28. DOI: https://doi.org/10.1075/jhp.13.1.01col.

Collins, A. M. & Loftus, E. F. (1975). A spreading-activation theory of semantic processing. *Psychological Review*, **82**(6), 407–428. DOI: https://doi.org/10.1037/0033-295X.82.6.407.

Coussé, E., Andersson, P. & Olofsson, J. (eds.). (2018). *Grammaticalization Meets Construction Grammar*. Amsterdam: John Benjamins. DOI: https://doi.org/10.1075/cal.21.

Croft, W. (2001). *Radical Construction Grammar: Syntactic Theory in Typological Perspective*. Oxford: Oxford University Press.

Croft, W. (2003). Lexical rules vs. constructions: A false dichotomy. In H. Cuyckens, T. Berg, R. Dirven, & K.-U. Panther (eds.), *Motivation in Language: Studies in Honor of Günter Radden*. Amsterdam: John Benjamins, pp. 49–68. DOI: https://doi.org/10.1075/cilt.243.07cro.

Croft, W. (2007). Construction Grammar. In D. Geeraerts & H. Cuyckens (eds.), *The Oxford Handbook of Cognitive Linguistics*. Oxford: Oxford University Press, pp. 463–508. DOI: https://doi.org/10.1093/oxfordhb/9780199738632.013.0018.

Croft, W. (2013). Radical Construction Grammar. In T. Hoffmann & G. Trousdale (eds.), *The Oxford Handbook of Construction Grammar*. Oxford: Oxford University Press, pp. 211–232. DOI: https://doi.org/10.1093/oxfordhb/9780195396683.013.0012.

Croft, W. (2020). *Ten Lectures on Construction Grammar and Typology*. Leiden: Brill.

Croft, W. (2022). On two mathematical representations for "semantic maps." *Zeitschrift Für Sprachwissenschaft*, **41**(1), 67–87.

Croft, W., & Cruse, D. A. (2004). *Cognitive Linguistics*. Cambridge: Cambridge University Press. DOI: https://doi.org/10.1017/CBO9780511803864.

Cummins, C. (2019). *Pragmatics*. Edinburgh: Edinburgh University Press. DOI: https://doi.org/10.1515/9781474440042.

Dąbrowska, E. (2008). Questions with long-distance dependencies: A usage-based perspective. *Cognitive Linguistics*, **19**(3), 391–425. DOI: https://doi.org/10.1515/COGL.2008.015.

Dąbrowska, E. (2009). Words as constructions. In V. Evans & S. Pourcel (eds.), *New Directions in Cognitive Linguistics*. Amsterdam: John Benjamins, pp. 201–223. DOI: https://doi.org/10.1075/hcp.24.16dab.

Dąbrowska, E. (2012). Different speakers, different grammars: Individual differences in native language attainment. *Linguistic Approaches to Bilingualism*, **2**(3), 219–253. DOI: https://doi.org/10.1075/lab.2.3.01dab.

Daelemans, W., De Smedt, K., & Gazdar, G. (1992). Inheritance in natural language processing. *Computational Linguistics*, **18**(2), 205–218.

Dancygier, B. & Vandelanotte, L. (2017). Internet memes as multimodal constructions. *Cognitive Linguistics*, **28**(3), 565–598. DOI: https://doi.org/10.1515/cog-2017-0074.

Davies, M. (2016–). Corpus of News on the Web (NOW). www.english-corpora.org/now/.

Dehaene, S. (2009). *Reading in the Brain: The Science and Evolution of a Human Invention*. New York: Viking.

De Knop, S. & Gilquin, G. (eds.). (2016). *Applied Construction Grammar*. Berlin: De Gruyter. DOI: https://doi.org/10.1515/9783110458268.

Deuchar, M. & Vihman, M. (2005). A radical approach to early mixed utterances. *International Journal of Bilingualism*, **9**(2), 137–157. DOI: https://doi.org/10.1177/13670069050090020201.

Diessel, H. (2013). Construction Grammar and first language acquisition. In Thomas Hoffmann & Graeme Trousdale (eds.), *The Oxford Handbook of Construction Grammar*. Oxford: Oxford University Press, pp. 346–364. DOI: https://doi.org/10.1093/oxfordhb/9780195396683.013.0019.

Diessel, H. (2015). Usage-based construction grammar. In E. Dąbrowska & D. Divjak (eds.), *Handbook of Cognitive Linguistics*. Berlin: De Gruyter, pp. 296–322. DOI: https://doi.org/10.1515/9783110292022-015.

Diessel, H. (2019). *The Grammar Network: How Linguistic Structure Is Shaped by Language Use*. Cambridge: Cambridge University Press. DOI: https://doi.org/10.1017/9781108671040.

Diessel, H. (2023). *The Constructicon: Taxonomies and Networks* (Elements in Construction Grammar). Cambridge: Cambridge University Press. DOI: https://doi.org/10.1017/9781009327848

Diessel, H., & Tomasello, M. (2005). A new look at the acquisition of relative clauses. *Language*, **81**(4), 882–906. DOI: https://doi.org/10.1353/lan.2005.0169.

Diewald, G. (2020). Paradigms lost – paradigms regained: Paradigms as hyper-constructions. In L. Sommerer & E. Smirnova (eds.), *Nodes and Networks in Diachronic Construction Grammar*. Amsterdam: John Benjamins, pp. 278–315. DOI: https://doi.org/10.1075/cal.27.08die

Di Sciullo, A. M. & Williams, E. (1987). *On the Definition of Word*. Cambridge, MA: MIT Press.

Divjak, D. (2019). *Frequency in Language: Memory, Attention and Learning*. Cambridge: Cambridge University Press. DOI: https://doi.org/10.1017/9781316084410.

Dodge, E. K. & Petruck, M. R. L. (2014). Representing caused motion in Embodied Construction Grammar. In Y. Artzi, T. Kwiatkowski, & J. Berant (eds.), *Proceedings of the ACL 2014 Workshop on Semantic Parsing.* Baltimore: Association for Computational Linguistics, pp. 39–44. DOI: https://doi.org/10.3115/v1/W14-2408.

Dominey, P. F., Mealier, A.-L., Pointeau, G., Mirliaz, S., & Finlayson, M. (2017). *Dynamic Construction Grammar and Steps Towards the Narrative Construction of Meaning.* Papers from the 2017 AAAI Spring Symposia SS-17-02, pp. 163–170.

Ellis, N. C. & Larsen-Freeman, D. (2006). Language emergence: Implications for applied linguistics – Introduction to the special issue. *Applied Linguistics*, **27**(4), 558–589. DOI: https://doi.org/10.1093/applin/aml028.

Ellis, N. C., Römer, U. & O'Donnell, M. B. (2016). *Usage-Based Approaches to Language Acquisition and Processing: Cognitive and Corpus Investigations of Construction Grammar.* Hoboken, NJ: Wiley.

Elman, J. L. (1990). Finding structure in time. *Cognitive Science*, **14**(2), 179–211. DOI: https://doi.org/10.1016/0364-0213(90)90002-E.

Eppe, M., Trott, S., Raghuram, V., Feldman, J., & Janin, A. (2016). Application-independent and integration-friendly natural language understanding. In C. Benzmüller, G. Sutcliffe, & R. Rojas (eds.),), *Global Conference on Artificial Intelligence (GCAI 2016).* EasyChair, pp. 340–352. DOI: https://doi.org/10.29007/npsn.

Evans, N. & Levinson, S. C. (2009). The myth of language universals: Language diversity and its importance for cognitive science. *Behavioral and Brain Sciences*, **32**, 429–492. DOI: https://doi.org/10.1017/S0140525X0999094X.

Feldman, J. A. (2006). *From Molecule to Metaphor: A Neural Theory of Language.* Cambridge, MA: MIT Press.

Feldman, J. A. (2020). Advances in Embodied Construction Grammar. *Constructions and Frames*, **12**(1), 149–169. DOI: https://doi.org/10.1075/cf.00038.fel.

Feldman, J., Dodge, E. & Bryant, J. (2015). Embodied Construction Grammar. In B. Heine & H. Narrog (eds.), *The Oxford Handbook of Linguistic Analysis*, 2nd ed. Oxford: Oxford University Press, pp. 121–146. DOI: https://doi.org/10.1093/oxfordhb/9780199677078.013.0006.

Fellbaum, C. (ed.). (1998). *WordNet: An Electronic Lexical Database.* Cambridge, MA: MIT Press.

Ferrer i Cancho, R. & Solé, R. V. (2001). The small world of human language. *Proceedings of the Royal Society of London. Series B: Biological Sciences*, **268**(1482), 2261–2265. DOI: https://doi.org/10.1098/rspb.2001.1800.

Ferrer i Cancho, R., Solé, R. V., & Köhler, R. (2004). Patterns in syntactic dependency networks. *Physical Review E*, **69**(5), 051915. DOI: https://doi.org/10.1103/PhysRevE.69.051915.

Feyaerts, K., Brône, G., & Oben, B. (2017). Multimodality in interaction. In B. Dancygier (ed.), *The Cambridge Handbook of Cognitive Linguistics*. Cambridge: Cambridge University Press, pp. 135–156. DOI: https://doi.org/10.1017/9781316339732.010.

Fillmore, C. J. (1968). The case for case. In E. Bach, R. T. Harms, & C. J. Fillmore (eds.), *Universals in Linguistic Theory*. London: Holt, Rinehart & Winston, pp. 1–88.

Fillmore, C. J. (1988). The mechanisms of "Construction Grammar." *Berkeley Linguistics Society*, **14**, 35–55.

Fillmore, C. J. (2013). Berkeley Construction Grammar. In T. Hoffmann & G. Trousdale (eds.), *The Oxford Handbook of Construction Grammar*. Oxford: Oxford University Press, pp. 110–132. DOI: https://doi.org/10.1093/oxfordhb/9780195396683.013.0007.

Fillmore, C. J., & Kay, P. (1993). *Construction Grammar Coursebook*. Berkeley: University of California, Berkeley.

Fillmore, C. J., Kay, P., & O'Connor, M. C. (1988). Regularity and idiomaticity in grammatical constructions: The case of *let alone*. *Language*, **64**(3), 501–538. DOI: https://doi.org/10.2307/414531

Fillmore, C. J., Lee-Goldman, R. R., & Rhomieux, R. (2012). The FrameNet constructicon. In H. C. Boas & I. A. Sag (eds.), *Sign-Based Construction Grammar*. Stanford: CSLI Publications, pp. 283–322.

Fischer, K., & Alm, M. (2013). A radical construction grammar perspective on the modal particle-discourse particle distinction. In L. Degand, B. Cornillie, & P. Pietrandrea (eds.), *Discourse Markers and Modal Particles: Categorization and Description*. Amsterdam: John Benjamins, pp. 47–88.

Flach, S., Kopf, K. & Stefanowitsch, A. (2018). Skandale und Skandälchen kontrastiv: Das Konfix -*gate* im Deutschen und Englischen. In R. Heuser & M. Schmuck (eds.), *Sonstige Namenarten: Stiefkinder der Onomastik*. Berlin: De Gruyter, pp. 239–268.

Fried, M. (2021). Discourse-referential patterns as a network of grammatical constructions. *Constructions and Frames*, **13**(1), 21–54. DOI: https://doi.org/10.1075/cf.00046.fri.

Fried, M. & Östman, J.-O. (2004). Construction Grammar: A thumbnail sketch. In M. Fried & J.-O. Östman (eds.), *Construction Grammar in a Cross-Language Perspective*. Amsterdam: John Benjamins, pp. 11–86. DOI: https://doi.org/10.1075/cal.2.02fri.

Gahl, S. & Plag, I. (2019). Spelling errors in English derivational suffixes reflect morphological boundary strength: A case study. *The Mental Lexicon*, **14**(1), 1–36. DOI: https://doi.org/10.1075/ml.19002.gah.

Gazdar, G., Klein, E., Pullum, G. K., & Sag, I. A. (1985). *Generalized Phrase Structure Grammar*. Cambridge, MA: Harvard University Press.

Geyer, K., Bick, E., & Kleene, A. (2022). "I am no racist but . . .": A corpus-based analysis of xenophobic hate speech constructions in Danish and German social media discourse. In N. Knoblock (ed.), *The Grammar of Hate*. Cambridge: Cambridge University Press, pp. 241–261. DOI: https://doi.org/10.1017/9781108991841.013.

Goldberg, A. E. (1995). *Constructions: A Construction Grammar Approach to Argument Structure*. Chicago: The University of Chicago Press.

Goldberg, A. E. (2005). Argument realization: The role of constructions, lexical semantics and discourse factors. In J.-O. Östman & M. Fried (eds.), *Construction Grammars: Cognitive Grounding and Theoretical Extensions*. Amsterdam: John Benjamins, pp. 17–43. DOI: https://doi.org/10.1075/cal.3.03gol.

Goldberg, A. E. (2006). *Constructions at Work: The Nature of Generalization in Language*. Oxford: Oxford University Press.

Goldberg, A. E. (2013). Constructionist approaches. In T. Hoffmann & G. Trousdale (eds.), *The Oxford Handbook of Construction Grammar*. Oxford: Oxford University Press, pp. 15–31. DOI: https://doi.org/10.1093/oxfordhb/9780195396683.013.0002.

Goldberg, A. E. (2019). *Explain Me This: Creativity, Competition, and the Partial Productivity of Constructions*. Princeton, NJ: Princeton University Press.

Goldin-Meadow, S., So, W. C., Ozyurek, A., & Mylander, C. (2008). The natural order of events: How speakers of different languages represent events nonverbally. *Proceedings of the National Academy of Sciences*, **105**(27), 9163–9168. DOI: https://doi.org/10.1073/pnas.0710060105.

Goldinger, S. D., Luce, P. A., & Pisoni, D. B. (1989). Priming lexical neighbors of spoken words: Effects of competition and inhibition. *Journal of Memory and Language*, **28**(5), 501–518. DOI: https://doi.org/10.1016/0749-596X(89)90009-0.

Gries, S. T. (2008). Dispersions and adjusted frequencies in corpora. *International Journal of Corpus Linguistics*, **13**(4), 403–437. DOI: https://doi.org/10.1075/ijcl.13.4.02gri.

Gries, S. T. (2011). Corpus data in usage-based linguistics: What's the right degree of granularity for the analysis of argument structure constructions? In M. Brdar, S. T. Gries, & M. Ž. Fuchs (eds.), *Cognitive Linguistics: Convergence and*

Expansion. Amsterdam: John Benjamins, pp. 237–256. DOI: https://doi.org/10
.1075/hcp.32.15gri.

Gries, S. T. (2015). More (old and new) misunderstandings of collostructional
analysis: On Schmid and Küchenhoff (2013). *Cognitive Linguistics*, **26**(3),
505–536. DOI: https://doi.org/10.1515/cog-2014-0092.

Gries, S. T. & Stefanowitsch, A. (2004). Extending collostructional analysis:
A corpus-based perspective on "alternations." *International Journal of
Corpus Linguistics*, **9**(1), 97–129. DOI: https://doi.org/10.1075/ijcl.9.1
.06gri.

Gries, S. T. & Wulff, S. (2009). Psycholinguistic and corpus-linguistic evidence
for L2 constructions. *Annual Review of Cognitive Linguistics*, **7**(1), 163–186.
DOI: https://doi.org/10.1075/arcl.7.07gri.

Harris, R. A. (2021). *The Linguistics Wars*, 2nd ed. Oxford: Oxford University
Press.

Hartmann, S. (2019). Compound worlds and metaphor landscapes: Affixoids,
allostructions, and higher-order generalizations. *Word Structure*, **12**(3),
297–333. DOI: https://doi.org/10.3366/word.2019.0151.

Hartmann, S. (2021). Diachronic Cognitive Linguistics: Past, present, and
future. *Yearbook of the German Cognitive Linguistics Association*, **9**(1),
1–34. DOI: https://doi.org/10.1515/gcla-2021-0001.

Hartmann, S. & Ungerer, T. (2023). Attack of the snowclones: A corpus-based
analysis of extravagant formulaic patterns. *Journal of Linguistics*. Advance
online publication. DOI: https://doi.org/10.1017/S0022226723000117.

Haspelmath, M. (1999). Why is grammaticalization irreversible? *Linguistics*,
37(6), 1043–1068. DOI: https://doi.org/10.1515/ling.37.6.1043.

Haspelmath, M. (2011). The indeterminacy of word segmentation and the
nature of morphology and syntax. *Folia Linguistica*, **45**(1), pp. 31–80.
DOI: https://doi.org/10.1515/flin.2011.002.

Hay, J. (2003). *Causes and Consequences of Word Structure*. New York:
Routledge.

Hay, J. & Baayen, H. (2002). Parsing and productivity. In G. E. Booij & J. van
Marle (eds.), *Yearbook of Morphology 2001*. Dordrecht: Kluwer,
pp. 203–235. DOI: https://doi.org/10.1007/978-94-017-3726-5_8.

Henrich, J., Heine, S. J., & Norenzayan, A. (2010). The weirdest people in the
world? *Behavioral and Brain Sciences*, **33**(2–3), pp. 61–83. DOI: https://doi
.org/10.1017/S0140525X0999152X.

Herbst, T. (2007). Valency complements or valency patterns? In T. Herbst &
K. Götz-Votteler (eds.), *Valency: Theoretical, Descriptive and Cognitive
Issues*. Berlin: De Gruyter, pp. 15–35. DOI: https://doi.org/10.1515
/9783110198775.1.15.

Herbst, T. (2011). The status of generalizations: Valency and argument structure constructions. *Zeitschrift für Anglistik und Amerikanistik*, **59**(4), 347–367. DOI: https://doi.org/10.1515/zaa-2011-0406.

Herbst, T. (2019). Constructicons – a new type of reference work? *Lexicographica*, **35**(2019), 3–14. DOI: https://doi.org/10.1515/lex-2019-0001.

Herbst, T. & Uhrig, P. (2020). The issue of specifying slots in argument structure constructions in terms of form and meaning. *Belgian Journal of Linguistics*, **34**, 135–147. DOI: https://doi.org/10.1075/bjl.00041.her.

Hilpert, M. (2013). *Constructional Change in English: Developments in Allomorphy, Word Formation, and Syntax*. Cambridge: Cambridge University Press. DOI: https://doi.org/10.1017/CBO9781139004206.

Hilpert, M. (2015). From *hand-carved* to *computer-based*: Noun-participle compounding and the upward strengthening hypothesis. *Cognitive Linguistics*, **26**(1), 113–147. DOI: https://doi.org/10.1515/cog-2014-0001.

Hilpert, M. (2016). Change in modal meanings: Another look at the shifting collocates of *may*. *Constructions and Frames*, **8**(1), 66–85. DOI: https://doi.org/10.1075/cf.8.1.05hil.

Hilpert, M. (2018). Three open questions in Diachronic Construction Grammar. In E. Coussé, P. Andersson, & J. Olofsson (eds.), *Grammaticalization Meets Construction Grammar*. Amsterdam: John Benjamins, pp. 21–39. DOI: https://doi.org/10.1075/cal.21.c2.

Hilpert, M. (2019). *Construction Grammar and Its Application to English*, 2nd ed. Edinburgh: Edinburgh University Press.

Hilpert, M. (2021). *Ten Lectures on Diachronic Construction Grammar*. Leiden: Brill.

Hilpert, M. & Diessel, H. (2017). Entrenchment in construction grammar. In H.-J. Schmid (ed.), *Entrenchment and the Psychology of Language Learning: How We Reorganize and Adapt Linguistic Knowledge*. Boston: APA & De Gruyter, pp. 57–74. DOI: https://doi.org/10.1037/15969-004.

Hilpert, M., & Perek, F. (2015). Meaning change in a petri dish: Constructions, semantic vector spaces, and motion charts. *Linguistics Vanguard*, **1**(1), 339–350.

Hilpert, M., & Perek, F. (2022). You don't get to see that every day: On the development of permissive *get*. *Constructions and Frames*, **14**(1), 13–40. DOI: https://doi.org/10.1075/cf.00056.hil.

Höder, S. (2012). Multilingual constructions: A diasystematic approach to common structures. In K. Braunmüller & C. Gabriel (eds.), *Multilingual Individuals and Multilingual Societies*. Amsterdam: John Benjamins, pp. 241–258. DOI: https://doi.org/10.1075/hsm.13.17hod.

Höder, S. (2014). Phonological elements and Diasystematic Construction Grammar. *Constructions and Frames*, **6**(2), 202–231. DOI: https://doi.org/10.1075/cf.6.2.04hod.

Hoffmann, T. (2011). *Preposition Placement in English: A Usage-Based Approach*. Cambridge: Cambridge University Press. DOI: https://doi.org/10.1017/CBO9780511933868.

Hoffmann, T. (2017a). Construction Grammars. In B. Dancygier (ed.), *The Cambridge Handbook of Cognitive Linguistics*. Cambridge: Cambridge University Press, pp. 310–329. DOI: https://doi.org/10.1017/9781316339732.020.

Hoffmann, T. (2017b). From constructions to Construction Grammars. In B. Dancygier (ed.), *The Cambridge Handbook of Cognitive Linguistics*. Cambridge: Cambridge University Press, pp. 284–309. DOI: https://doi.org/10.1017/9781316339732.019.

Hoffmann, T. (2018). Creativity and Construction Grammar: Cognitive and psychological issues. *Zeitschrift für Anglistik und Amerikanistik*, **66**(3), 259–276. DOI: https://doi.org/10.1515/zaa-2018-0024.

Hoffmann, T. (2020). What would it take for us to abandon Construction Grammar? Falsifiability, confirmation bias and the future of the constructionist enterprise. *Belgian Journal of Linguistics*, **34**, 148–160. DOI: https://doi.org/10.1075/bjl.00042.hof.

Hoffmann, T. (2022). *Construction Grammar: The Structure of English*. Cambridge: Cambridge University Press.

Hoffmann, T. & Trousdale, G. (eds.). (2013). *The Oxford Handbook of Construction Grammar*. Oxford: Oxford University Press. DOI: https://doi.org/10.1093/oxfordhb/9780195396683.001.0001.

Hoffmann, T. & Trousdale, G. (2022). On multiple paths and change in the language network. *Zeitschrift für Anglistik und Amerikanistik*, **70**(3), 359–382. DOI: https://doi.org/10.1515/zaa-2022-2071.

Hölzl, A. (2018). Constructionalization areas: The case of negation in Manchu. In E. Coussé, P. Andersson, & J. Olofsson (eds.), *Grammaticalization Meets Construction Grammar*. Amsterdam: John Benjamins, pp. 241–276. DOI: https://doi.org/10.1075/cal.21.c9.

Hopper, P. (1987). Emergent grammar. *Berkeley Linguistics Society*, **10**, 139–157.

Hudson, R. (2007). *Language Networks: The New Word Grammar*. Oxford: Oxford University Press.

Hudson, R. (2015). Review of Rolf Kreyer, *The nature of rules, regularities and units in language: A network model of the language system and of language use. Journal of Linguistics*, **51**(3), 692–696. DOI: https://doi.org/10.1017 /S002222671500016X.

Ibbotson, P., Salnikov, V., & Walker, R. (2019). A dynamic network analysis of emergent grammar. *First Language*, **39**(6), 652–680. DOI: https://doi.org/10 .1177/0142723719869562.

Israel, M. (1996). The *way* constructions grow. In A. Goldberg (ed.), *Conceptual Structure, Discourse and Language*. Stanford, CA: CSLI, pp. 217–230.

Jackendoff, R. (2002). *Foundations of Language: Brain, Meaning, Grammar, Evolution*. Oxford: Oxford University Press.

Jackendoff, R., & Audring, J. (2020). *The Texture of the Lexicon: Relational Morphology and the Parallel Architecture*. Oxford: Oxford University Press.

Janda, L. A. (2013). Quantitative methods in cognitive linguistics: An introduction. In L. A. Janda (ed.), *Cognitive Linguistics – The Quantitative Turn: The Essential Reader*. Berlin: De Gruyter, pp. 1–32. DOI: https://doi.org/10.1515 /9783110335255.1.

Janda, L. A., Lyashevskaya, O., Nesset, T., Rakhilina, E., & Typers, F. M. (2018). A constructicon for Russian: Filling in the gaps. In B. Lyngfelt, L. Borin, K. Ohara, & T. T. Torrent (eds.), *Constructicography: Constructicon Development across Languages*. Amsterdam: John Benjamins, pp. 165–181. DOI: https://doi.org/10.1075/cal.22.06jan.

Jespersen, O. (1917). *Negation in English and Other Languages*. Copenhagen: Høst.

Kay, P. (1990). Even. *Linguistics and Philosophy*, **13**(1), 59–111. DOI: https:// doi.org/10.1007/BF00630517

Kay, P. & Fillmore, C. J. (1999). Grammatical constructions and linguistic generalizations: The *What's X doing Y?* construction. *Language*, **75**(1), 1–33. DOI: https://doi.org/10.2307/417472.

Keller, R. (1994). *Language Change: The Invisible Hand in Language*. London: Routledge.

Kendon, A. (2004). *Gesture: Visible Action as Utterance*. Cambridge: Cambridge University Press. DOI: https://doi.org/10.1017/CBO9780511807572.

Knight, K. (1989). Unification: A multidisciplinary survey. *ACM Computer Surveys*, **21**(1), 93–124. https://doi.org/10.1145/62029.62030.

Küchenhoff, H. & Schmid, H.-J. (2015). Reply to "More (old and new) misunderstandings of collostructional analysis: On Schmid & Küchenhoff" by Stefan Th. Gries. *Cognitive Linguistics*, **26**(3), 537–547. DOI: https://doi .org/10.1515/cog-2015-0053.

Kuiper, K. & Haggo, D. (1984). Livestock auctions, oral poetry, and ordinary language. *Language in Society*, **13**(2), 205–234.

Lakoff, G. (1987). *Women, Fire, and Dangerous Things: What Categories Reveal about the Mind.* Chicago: The University of Chicago Press.

Lambrecht, K. (2004). On the interaction of information structure and formal structure in constructions: The case of French right-detached *comme*-N. In M. Fried & J.-O. Östman (eds.), *Construction Grammar in a Cross-Language Perspective.* Amsterdam: John Benjamins, pp. 157–199. DOI: https://doi.org/10.1075/cal.2.05lam

Langacker, R. W. (1987). *Foundations of Cognitive Grammar*, vol. 1: *Theoretical Prerequisites.* Stanford, CA: Stanford University Press.

Langacker, R. W. (1988). A usage-based model. In B. Rudzka-Ostyn (ed.), *Topics in Cognitive Linguistics.* Amsterdam: John Benjamins, pp. 127–161. DOI: https://doi.org/10.1075/cilt.50.06lan.

Langacker, R. W. (2005). Construction Grammars: Cognitive, radical, and less so. In M. S. Peña Cervel & F. J. de Ruiz Mendoza Ibáñez (eds.), *Cognitive Linguistics: Internal Dynamics and Interdisciplinary Interaction.* Berlin: De Gruyter, pp. 101–159.

Langacker, R. W. (2008). *Cognitive Grammar: A Basic Introduction.* Oxford: Oxford University Press.

Langacker, R. W. (2017). Entrenchment in cognitive grammar. In H.-J. Schmid (ed.), *Entrenchment and the Psychology of Language Learning: How We Reorganize and Adapt Linguistic Knowledge.* Boston: APA & De Gruyter, pp. 39–56. DOI: https://doi.org/10.1037/15969-003.

Langacker, R. W. (2019). Construal. In E. Dąbrowska & D. Divjak (eds.), *Cognitive Linguistics – Foundations of Language.* Berlin: De Gruyter, pp. 140–166. DOI: https://doi.org/10.1515/9783110626476-007.

Lanwer, J. P. (2017). Apposition: A multimodal construction? The multimodality of linguistic constructions in the light of usage-based theory. *Linguistics Vanguard*, **3**(s1). DOI: https://doi.org/10.1515/lingvan-2016-0071.

Leclercq, B. (2020). Semantics and pragmatics in Construction Grammar. *Belgian Journal of Linguistics*, **34**, 225–234. DOI: https://doi.org/10.1075/bjl.00048.lec.

Lenci, A. (2018). Distributional models of word meaning. *Annual Review of Linguistics*, **4**(1), 151–171. DOI: https://doi.org/10.1146/annurev-linguistics-030514-125254.

Lepic, R. & Occhino., C. 2018. A construction morphology approach to sign language analysis. In G. E. Booij (ed.), *The Construction of Words: Advances in Construction Morphology.* Berlin: Springer, pp. 141–172. DOI: https://doi.org/10.1007/978-3-319-74394-3_6.

Lorenz, D. (2020). Converging variations and the emergence of horizontal links: *To*-contraction in American English. In L. Sommerer & E. Smirnova (eds.), *Nodes and networks in Diachronic Construction Grammar*. Amsterdam: John Benjamins, pp. 243–274. DOI: https://doi.org/10.1075/cal .27.07lor.

Losiewicz, B. (1992). The effect of duration on linguistic morphology. (Ph.D. dissertation, University of Texas, Austin.)

Lyngfelt, B., Borin, L., Ohara, K., & Torrent, T. T. (eds.). (2018). *Constructicography: Constructicon Development across Languages*. Amsterdam: John Benjamins. https://doi.org/10.1075/cal.22.

MacWhinney, B. (2019). Emergentism. In E. Dąbrowska & D. Divjak (eds.), *Cognitive Linguistics: Key Topics*. Berlin: De Gruyter, pp. 275–294. DOI: https://doi.org/10.1515/9783110626438-014.

Manning, C. D., Clark, K., Hewitt, J., Khandelwal, U., & Levy, O. (2020). Emergent linguistic structure in artificial neural networks trained by self-supervision. *Proceedings of the National Academy of Sciences*, **117** (48), 30046–30054. DOI: https://doi.org/10.1073/pnas.1907367117.

Matlock, T. & Winter, B. (2015). Experimental semantics. In B. Heine & H. Narrog (eds.), *The Oxford Handbook of Linguistic Analysis*. Oxford: Oxford University Press, pp. 771–790. DOI: https://doi.org/10.1093 /oxfordhb/9780199677078.013.0037.

McNeill, D. (2011). Gesture. In P. C. Hogan (ed.), *The Cambridge Encyclopedia of the Language Sciences*. Cambridge: Cambridge University Press, pp. 344–346.

McNeill, D. (2016). *Why We Gesture: The Surprising Role of Hand Movements in Communication*. Cambridge: Cambridge University Press. DOI: https:// doi.org/10.1017/CBO9781316480526.

Meletis, D. (2020). *The Nature of Writing a Theory of Grapholinguistics*. Brest: Fluxus Editions. https://doi.org/10.36824/2020-meletis.

Meletis, D. & Dürscheid, C. (2022). *Writing Systems and Their Use: An Overview of Grapholinguistics*. Berlin: De Gruyter. DOI: https://doi.org/10 .1515/9783110757835.

Meyer, D. E. & Schvaneveldt, R. W. (1971). Facilitation in recognizing pairs of words: Evidence of a dependence between retrieval operations. *Journal of Experimental Psychology*, **90**(2), 227–234. DOI: https://doi.org/10.1037 /h0031564.

Meyer, D. E., Schvaneveldt, R. W., & Ruddy, M. G. (1974). Functions of graphemic and phonemic codes in visual word-recognition. *Memory & Cognition*, **2**(2), 309–321. DOI: https://doi.org/10.3758/BF03209002.

Michaelis, L. A. (1993). Toward a grammar of aspect: The case of the English perfect construction. (Ph.D. dissertation, University of California, Berkeley.)

Michaelis, L. A. (2013). Sign-based Construction Grammar. In T. Hoffmann & G. Trousdale (eds.), *The Oxford Handbook of Construction Grammar*. Oxford: Oxford University Press, pp. 133–152. DOI: https://doi.org/10.1093/oxfordhb/9780195396683.013.0008

Michaelis, L. A. (2015). Sign-Based Construction Grammar. In B. Heine & H. Narrog, eds., *The Oxford Handbook of Linguistic Analysis*, 2nd edn. Oxford: Oxford University Press, pp. 147–166. https://doi.org/10.1093/oxfordhb/9780199677078.013.0007.

Michaelis, L. A. & Lambrecht, K. (1996). Toward a construction-based theory of language function: The case of nominal extraposition. *Language*, **72**(2), 215–247. DOI: https://doi.org/10.2307/416650.

Mok, E. H. (2009). Contextual bootstrapping for grammar learning. (Ph.D. dissertation, University of California, Berkeley.)

Mosegaard Hansen, M.-B. (2011). Negative cycles and grammaticalization. In B. Heine & H. Narrog (eds.), *The Oxford Handbook of Grammaticalization*. Oxford: Oxford University Press, pp. 570–579. DOI: https://doi.org/10.1093/oxfordhb/9780199586783.013.0046.

Neef, M. (2015). Writing systems as modular objects: Proposals for theory design in grapholinguistics. *Open Linguistics*, **1**(1). DOI: https://doi.org/10.1515/opli-2015-0026.

Neels, J. (2020). Lifespan change in grammaticalisation as frequency-sensitive automation: William Faulkner and the *let alone* construction. *Cognitive Linguistics*, **31**(2), 339–365. DOI: https://doi.org/10.1515/cog-2019-0020.

Nevens, J., Eecke, P. V., & Beuls, K. (2019). Computational construction grammar for visual question answering. *Linguistics Vanguard*, **5**(1). DOI: https://doi.org/10.1515/lingvan-2018-0070.

Nölle, J. & Galantucci, B. (2023). Experimental semiotics: Past, present, and future. In A. M. García & A. Ibáñez (eds.), *The Routledge Handbook of Semiosis and the Brain*. New York: Routledge, pp. 66–81. DOI: https://doi.org/10.4324/9781003051817-6.

Norde, M. & Sippach, S. (2019). *Nerdalicious scientainment*: A network analysis of English libfixes. *Word Structure*, **12**(3), 353–384. DOI: https://doi.org/10.3366/word.2019.0153.

Pawley, A. (1985). On speech formulas and linguistic competence. *Lenguas Modernas*, **12**, 84–104.

Percillier, M. (2020). Allostructions, homostructions or a constructional family? Changes in the network of secondary predicate constructions in Middle English. In L. Sommerer & E. Smirnova (eds.), *Nodes and Networks in Diachronic Construction Grammar*. Amsterdam: John Benjamins, pp. 213–242. DOI: https://doi.org/10.1075/cal.27.06per.

Perek, F. (2012). Alternation-based generalizations are stored in the mental grammar: Evidence from a sorting task experiment. *Cognitive Linguistics*, **23** (3), 601–635. DOI: https://doi.org/10.1515/cog-2012-0018.

Perek, F. (2015). *Argument Structure in Usage-Based Construction Grammar.* Amsterdam: John Benjamins. DOI: https://doi.org/10.1075/cal.17.

Perek, F. (2016). Using distributional semantics to study syntactic productivity in diachrony: A case study. *Linguistics*, **54**(1), 149–188. DOI: https://doi.org /10.1515/ling-2015-0043.

Perek, F., & Goldberg, A. E. (2015). Generalizing beyond the input: The functions of the constructions matter. *Journal of Memory and Language*, **84**, 108–127. DOI: https://doi.org/10.1016/j.jml.2015.04.006.

Perek, F., & Patten, A. L. (2019). Towards an English Constructicon using patterns and frames. *International Journal of Corpus Linguistics*, **24**(3), 354–384. DOI: https://doi.org/10.1075/ijcl.00016.per.

Petré, P., & Anthonissen, L. (2020). Individuality in complex systems: A constructionist approach. *Cognitive Linguistics*, **31**(2), 185–212. DOI: https://doi.org/10.1515/cog-2019-0033.

Petruck, M. R. L. (2022). Frame semantics. In J. Verschueren & J.-O. Östman (eds.), *Handbook of Pragmatics: Manual*, 2nd ed. Amsterdam: John Benjamins, pp. 592–601. https://doi.org/10.1075/hop.m2.fra1.

Pijpops, D. (2020). What is an alternation? Six answers. *Belgian Journal of Linguistics*, **34**, 283–294. DOI: https://doi.org/10.1075/bjl.00053.pij.

Pijpops, D. & Van de Velde, F. (2016). Constructional contamination: How does it work and how do we measure it? *Folia Linguistica*, **50**(2), 543–581. DOI: https://doi.org/10.1515/flin-2016-0020.

Pinker, S. (1994). *The Language Instinct: How the Mind Creates Language.* New York: Morrow.

Pleyer, M, Lepic, R., & Hartmann, S. (2022). Compositionality in different modalities: A view from usage-based linguistics. *International Journal of Primatology*. Advance online publication. DOI: https://doi.org/10.1007 /s10764-022-00330-x.

Pollard, C. & Sag, I. A. (1987). *Information-Based Syntax and Semantics.* Stanford, CA: CSLI Publications.

Pulvermüller, F. (2010). Brain embodiment of syntax and grammar: Discrete combinatorial mechanisms spelt out in neuronal circuits. *Brain and Language*, **112**(3), 167–179. DOI: https://doi.org/10.1016/j.bandl.2009.08.002.

Pulvermüller, F., Cappelle, B., & Shtyrov, Y. (2013). Brain basis of meaning, words, constructions, and grammar. In T. Hoffmann & G. Trousdale, eds., *The Oxford Handbook of Construction Grammar.* Oxford: Oxford University

Press, pp. 397–415. https://doi.org/10.1093/oxfordhb/9780195396683.013.0022.

Rumelhart, D. E. & McClelland, J. L. (1986). On learning the past tenses of English verbs. In D. E. Rumelhart, J. L. McClelland, & the PDP Research Group (eds.), *Parallel Distributed Processing: Explorations in the Microstructure of Cognition*, Vol. 2: *Psychological and Biological Models*. Cambridge, MA: MIT Press, pp. 216–271.

Sag, I. A. (2010). English filler-gap constructions. *Language*, **86**(3), 486–545.

Sag, I. A. (2012). Sign-Based Construction Grammar: An informal synopsis. In H. C. Boas & I. A. Sag (eds.), *Sign-Based Construction Grammar*. Stanford, CA: CSLI, pp. 61–188.

Sampson, G. (2016). Two ideas of creativity. In M. Hinton, ed., *Evidence, Experiment and Argument in Linguistics and Philosophy of Language*. Bern: Peter Lang, pp. 15–26.

Schmid, H.-J. (2017a). A framework for understanding linguistic entrenchment and its psychological foundations. In H.-J. Schmid (ed.), *Entrenchment and the Psychology of Language Learning: How We Reorganize and Adapt Linguistic Knowledge*. Boston: APA & De Gruyter, pp. 9–36. DOI: https://doi.org/10.1037/15969-002.

Schmid, H.-J. (ed.). (2017b). *Entrenchment and the Psychology of Language Learning: How We Reorganize and Adapt Linguistic Knowledge*. Boston: APA & De Gruyter. DOI: https://doi.org/10.1037/15969-000.

Schmid, H.-J. (2020). *The Dynamics of the Linguistic System: Usage, Conventionalization, and Entrenchment*. Oxford: Oxford University Press.

Schmid, H.-J., & Mantlik, A. (2015). Entrenchment in historical corpora? Reconstructing dead authors' minds from their usage profiles. *Anglia*, **133**(4), 583–623. DOI: https://doi.org/10.1515/ang-2015-0056.

Schmid, H.-J. & Küchenhoff, H. (2013). Collostructional analysis and other ways of measuring lexicogrammatical attraction: Theoretical premises, practical problems and cognitive underpinnings. *Cognitive Linguistics*, **24**(3), 531–577. DOI: https://doi.org/10.1515/cog-2013-0018.

Schneider, N. (2010). Computational cognitive morphosemantics: Modeling morphological compositionality in Hebrew verbs with Embodied Construction Grammar. *Berkeley Linguistics Society*, **36**(1), 353–367.

Schönefeld, D. (2011). On evidence and the convergence of evidence in linguistic research. In D. Schönefeld (ed.), *Converging Evidence: Methodological and Theoretical Issues for Linguistic Research*. Amsterdam: John Benjamins, pp. 1–31. DOI: https://doi.org/10.1075/hcp.33.03sch.

Schoonjans, S. (2017). Multimodal Construction Grammar issues are Construction Grammar issues. *Linguistics Vanguard*, **3**(s1). DOI: https://doi .org/10.1515/lingvan-2016-0050.

Shieber, S. (1986). *An Introduction to Unification-Based Approaches to Grammar*. Stanford, CA: CSLI Publications.

Siew, C. S. Q. (2018). The orthographic similarity structure of English words: Insights from network science. *Applied Network Science*, **3**(1), 1–18. DOI: https://doi.org/10.1007/s41109-018-0068-1.

Smirnova, E. (2021). Horizontal links within and between paradigms: The constructional network of reported directives in German. In M. Hilpert, B. Cappelle, & I. Depraetere (eds.), *Modality and Diachronic Construction Grammar*. Amsterdam: John Benjamins, pp. 185–218. DOI: https://doi.org /10.1075/cal.32.07smi.

Smirnova, E. & Sommerer, L. (2020). Introduction: The nature of the node and the network: Open questions in Diachronic Construction Grammar. In L. Sommerer & E. Smirnova (eds.), *Nodes and Networks in Diachronic Construction Grammar*. Amsterdam: John Benjamins, pp. 1–42. DOI: https://doi.org/10.1075/cal.27.int.

Sommerer, L. (2018). *Article Emergence in Old English: A Constructionalist Perspective*. Berlin: De Gruyter. DOI: https://doi.org/10.1515/9783110541052.

Sommerer, L. (2020). Constructionalization, constructional competition and constructional death: Investigating the demise of Old English POSS DEM constructions. In L. Sommerer & E. Smirnova (eds.), *Nodes and Networks in Diachronic Construction Grammar*. Amsterdam: John Benjamins, pp. 69–103. DOI: https://doi.org/10.1075/cal.27.02som.

Sommerer, L. & Baumann, A. (2021). Of absent mothers, strong sisters and peculiar daughters: The constructional network of English NPN constructions. *Cognitive Linguistics*, **32**(1), 97–131. DOI: https://doi.org/10 .1515/cog-2020-0013.

Sommerer, L. & Smirnova, E. (eds.). (2020). *Nodes and Networks in Diachronic Construction Grammar*. Amsterdam: John Benjamins. DOI: https://doi.org/10 .1075/cal.27.

Standing, W. & Petré, P. (2021). Exploiting convention: Lifespan change and generational incrementation in the development of cleft constructions. In K. V. Beaman & I. Buchstaller (eds.), *Language Variation and Language Change across the Lifespan: Theoretical and Empirical Perspectives from Panel Studies*. New York: Routledge, pp. 141–163.

Steels, L. (2011). Introducing Fluid Construction Grammar. In L. Steels (ed.), *Design Patterns in Fluid Construction Grammar*. Amsterdam: John Benjamins, pp. 3–30. DOI: https://doi.org/10.1075/cal.11.03ste.

Steels, L. (2012). *Experiments in Cultural Language Evolution*. Amsterdam: John Benjamins. DOI: https://doi.org/10.1075/ais.3.

Steels, L. (2013). Fluid Construction Grammar. In T. Hoffmann & G. Trousdale (eds.), *The Oxford Handbook of Construction Grammar*. Oxford: Oxford University Press, pp. 155–167. DOI: https://doi.org/10.1093/oxfordhb/9780195396683.013.0009.

Steels, L. (2017). Basics of Fluid Construction Grammar. *Constructions and Frames*, **9**(2), 178–225. DOI: https://doi.org/10.1075/cf.00002.ste.

Steels, L., & Hild, M. (eds.). (2012). *Language grounding in robots*. New York: Springer. DOI: https://doi.org/10.1007/978-1-4614-3064-3.

Steels, L., & Szathmáry, E. (2016). Fluid Construction Grammar as a biological system. *Linguistics Vanguard*, **2**(1),1–19.

Stefanowitsch, A. (2011). Argument structure: Item-based or distributed? *Zeitschrift für Anglistik und Amerikanistik*, **59**(4), 369–386. DOI: https://doi.org/10.1515/zaa-2011-0407.

Stefanowitsch, A. (2013). Collostructional analysis. In T. Hoffmann & G. Trousdale, eds., *The Oxford Handbook of Construction Grammar*. Oxford: Oxford University Press, pp. 290–306. https://doi.org/10.1093/oxfordhb/9780195396683.013.0016.

Stefanowitsch, A. & Gries, S. T. (2003). Collostructions: Investigating the interaction of words and constructions. *International Journal of Corpus Linguistics*, **8**(2), 209–243. DOI: https://doi.org/10.1075/ijcl.8.2.03ste.

Stefanowitsch, A. & Gries, S. T. (2005). Covarying collexemes. *Corpus Linguistics and Linguistic Theory*, **1**(1), 1–43. DOI: https://doi.org/10.1515/cllt.2005.1.1.1.

Steyvers, M. & Tenenbaum, J. B. (2005). The large-scale structure of semantic networks: Statistical analyses and a model of semantic growth. *Cognitive Science*, **29**(1), 41–78. DOI: https://doi.org/10.1207/s15516709cog2901_3.

Szcześniak, K. & Pachoł, M. (2015). What? Me, lie? The form and reading of the incredulity response construction. *Constructions*, **10**, 1–10. DOI: https://doi.org/10.24338/CONS-470.

Talmy, L. (2007). Foreword. In M. Gonzales-Marquez, I. Mittelberg, S. Coulson, & M. J. Spivey (eds.), *Methods in Cognitive Linguistics*. Amsterdam: John Benjamins, pp. xi–xxi. DOI: https://doi.org/10.1075/hcp.18.03tal.

Taylor, J. R. (2012). *The Mental Corpus: How Language is Represented in the Mind*. Oxford: Oxford University Press.

Tesnière, L. (1959). *Éléments de syntaxe structurale*. Paris: Klincksieck.

Tomasello, M. (1992). *First Verbs: A Case Study of Early Grammatical Development*. Cambridge: Cambridge University Press. DOI: https://doi.org/10.1017/CBO9780511527678.

Tomasello, M. (2003). *Constructing a Language: A Usage-Based Theory of Language Acquisition*. Cambridge, MA: Harvard University Press.

Tomasello, M. & Lieven, E. (2008). Children's first language acquisition from a usage-based perspective. In P. Robinson & N. J. Ellis (eds.), *Handbook of Cognitive Linguistics and Second Language Acquisition*. New York: Routledge, pp. 168–196.

Torrent, T. T. (2015). The constructional convergence and the construction network reconfiguration hypotheses: On the relation between inheritance and change. In J. Barðdal, E. Smirnova, L. Sommerer, & S. Gildea (eds.), *Diachronic Construction Grammar*. Amsterdam: John Benjamins, pp. 173–212. DOI: https://doi.org/10.1075/cal.18.06tor.

Torrent, T. T., da Silva Matos, E. E., Lage, L. et al. (2018). Towards continuity between the lexicon and the constructicon in FrameNet Brasil. In B. Lyngfelt, L. Borin, K. Ohara, & T. T. Torrent (eds.), *Constructicography: Constructicon Development across Languages*. Amsterdam: John Benjamins, pp. 107–140. DOI: https://doi.org/10.1075/cal.22.04tor.

Traugott, E. C. (2022). *Discourse Structuring Markers in English: A Historical Constructionalist Perspective on Pragmatics*. Amsterdam: John Benjamins. DOI: https://doi.org/10.1075/cal.33.

Traugott, E. C. & Trousdale, G. (2013). *Constructionalization and Constructional Changes*. Oxford: Oxford University Press.

Trousdale, G. (2012). Theory and data in diachronic Construction Grammar: The case of the *what with* construction. *Studies in Language*, **36**(3), 576–602. DOI: https://doi.org/10.1075/sl.36.3.05tro.

Turner, M. (2019). Blending in language and communication. In E. Dąbrowska & D. Divjak (eds.), *Cognitive Linguistics – Foundations of Language*. Berlin: De Gruyter, pp. 245–270. https://doi.org/10.1515/9783110626476-011.

Ungerer, T. (2021). Using structural priming to test links between constructions: English caused-motion and resultative sentences inhibit each other. *Cognitive Linguistics*, **32**(3), 389–420. DOI: https://doi.org/10.1515/cog-2020-0016.

Ungerer, T. (2022). Structural priming in the grammatical network: A study of English argument structure construction. (Ph.D. dissertation, University of Edinburgh.)

Ungerer, T. (2023). A gradient notion of constructionhood. *Constructions*, Special Issue "35 Years of Constructions," 1–20. DOI: https://doi.org/10.24338/cons-543

Ungerer, T. (in press). Vertical and horizontal links in constructional networks: Two sides of the same coin? *Constructions and Frames*.

Ungerer, T., & Hartmann, S. (2020). Delineating extravagance: Assessing speakers' perceptions of imaginative constructional patterns. *Belgian Journal of Linguistics*, **34**, 345–356. DOI: https://doi.org/10.1075/bjl.00058.ung.

Van de Velde, F. (2014). Degeneracy: The maintenance of constructional networks. In R. Boogaart, T. Colleman, & G. Rutten (eds.), *Extending the Scope of Construction Grammar*. Berlin: De Gruyter, pp. 141–179. DOI: https://doi.org/10.1515/9783110366273.141.

Van Eecke, P. (2017). Robust processing of the Dutch verb phrase. *Constructions and Frames*, **9**(2), 226–250. DOI: https://doi.org/10.1075/bct.106.cf.00003.van.

Van Trijp, R. (2014). Long-distance dependencies without filler–gaps: A cognitive-functional alternative in Fluid Construction Grammar. *Language and Cognition*, **6**(2), 242–270. DOI: https://doi.org/10.1017/langcog.2014.8.

Van Trijp, R. (2017). How a Construction Grammar account solves the auxiliary controversy. *Constructions and Frames*, **9**(2), 251–277. DOI: https://doi.org/10.1075/cf.00004.van.

Van Trijp, R. (2020). Making good on a promise: Multidimensional constructions. *Belgian Journal of Linguistics*, **34**, 357–370. DOI: https://doi.org/10.1075/bjl.00059.tri.

Van Trijp, R., Beuls, K., & Van Eecke, P. (2022). The FCG Editor: An innovative environment for engineering computational construction grammars. *PLOS ONE*, **17**(6), e0269708. DOI: https://doi.org/10.1371/journal.pone.0269708.

Vihman, M. & Croft, W. (2007). Phonological development: Toward a "radical" templatic phonology. *Linguistics*, **45**(4), 683–725. DOI: https://doi.org/10.1515/LING.2007.021.

Vitevitch, M. S. (2008). What can graph theory tell us about word learning and lexical retrieval? *Journal of Speech, Language, and Hearing Research*, **51**(2), 408–422. DOI: https://doi.org/10.1044/1092-4388(2008/030).

Walsh, O. (2021). Introduction: In the shadow of the standard. Standard language ideology and attitudes towards "non-standard" varieties and usages. *Journal of Multilingual and Multicultural Development*, **42**(9), 773–782. DOI: https://doi.org/10.1080/01434632.2020.1813146.

Wasserscheidt, P. (2015). Bilinguales Sprechen: Ein konstruktionsgrammatischer Ansatz. (Ph.D. dissertation, Free University of Berlin.)

Wasserscheidt, P. (2021). A usage-based approach to "language" in language contact. *Applied Linguistics Review*, **12**(2), 279–298. DOI: https://doi.org/10.1515/applirev-2019-0032.

Willaert, T., Van Eecke, P., Beuls, K., & Steels, L. (2020). Building social media observatories for monitoring online opinion dynamics. *Social Media + Society*, **6**(2), 1–12. https://doi.org/10.1177/2056305119898778.

Willems, K. (2012). Intuition, introspection and observation in linguistic inquiry. *Language Sciences*, **34**(6), 665–681. DOI: https://doi.org/10.1016/j.langsci.2012.04.008.

Willich, A. (2022). *Konstruktionssemantik: Frames in gebrauchsbasierter Konstruktionsgrammatik und Konstruktikographie.* Berlin: De Gruyter. DOI: https://doi.org/10.1515/9783110762341.

Wulff, S. (2008). *Rethinking Idiomaticity: A Usage-Based Approach.* London: Continuum.

Wulff, S. (2013). Words and idioms. In T. Hoffmann & G. Trousdale (eds.), *The Oxford Handbook of Construction Grammar.* Oxford: Oxford University Press, pp. 274–289. DOI: https://doi.org/10.1093/oxfordhb/9780195396683.013.0015.

Zehentner, E. (2019). *Competition in Language Change: The Rise of the English Dative Alternation.* Berlin: De Gruyter. DOI: https://doi.org/10.1515/9783110633856.

Zeschel, A. (2009). What's (in) a construction? Complete inheritance vs. full-entry models. In V. Evans & S. Pourcel (eds.), *New Directions in Cognitive Linguistics.* Amsterdam: John Benjamins, pp. 185–200. DOI: https://doi.org/10.1075/hcp.24.15zes.

Ziegler, J. & Snedeker, J. (2018). How broad are thematic roles? Evidence from structural priming. *Cognition,* **179**, 221–240. https://doi.org/10.1016/j.cognition.2018.06.019.

Ziem, A. (2017). Do we really need a Multimodal Construction Grammar? *Linguistics Vanguard,* **3**(s1). DOI: https://doi.org/10.1515/lingvan-2016-0095.

Ziem, A., Flick, J., & Sandkühler, P. (2019). The German Constructicon Project: Framework, methodology, resources. *Lexicographica,* **35**(2019), 15–40. DOI: https://doi.org/10.1515/lex-2019-0003.

Ziem, A. & Lasch, A. (2013). *Konstruktionsgrammatik: Konzepte und Grundlagen gebrauchsbasierter Ansätze.* Berlin: De Gruyter. DOI: https://doi.org/10.1515/9783110295641.

Zima, E. (2014). Gibt es multimodale Konstruktionen? Eine Studie zu [V(motion) in circles] und [all the way from X PREP Y]. *Gesprächsforschung,* **15**, 1–48.

Cambridge Elements ⁼

Construction Grammar

Thomas Hoffmann
Catholic University of Eichstätt-Ingolstadt

Thomas Hoffmann is Full Professor and Chair of English Language and Linguistics at the Catholic University of Eichstätt-Ingolstadt as well as Furong Scholar Distinguished Chair Professor of Hunan Normal University. His main research interests are usage-based Construction Grammar, language variation and change and linguistic creativity. He has published widely in international journals such as *Cognitive Linguistics, English Language and Linguistics*, and *English World-Wide*. His monographs *Preposition Placement in English* (2011) and *English Comparative Correlatives: Diachronic and Synchronic Variation at the Lexicon-Syntax Interface* (2019) were both published by Cambridge University Press. His textbook on *Construction Grammar: The Structure of English* (2022) as well as an Element on *The Cognitive Foundation of Post-colonial Englishes: Construction Grammar as the Cognitive Theory for the Dynamic Model* (2021) have also both been published with Cambridge University Press. He is also co-editor (with Graeme Trousdale) of *The Oxford Handbook of Construction Grammar* (2013, Oxford University Press).

Alexander Bergs
Osnabrück University

Alexander Bergs joined the Institute for English and American Studies at Osnabrück University, Germany, in 2006 when he became Full Professor and Chair of English Language and Linguistics. His research interests include, among others, language variation and change, constructional approaches to language, the role of context in language, the syntax/pragmatics interface, and cognitive poetics. His works include several authored and edited books (*Social Networks and Historical Sociolinguistics, Modern Scots, Contexts and Constructions, Constructions and Language Change*), a short textbook on *Synchronic English Linguistics*, one on *Understanding Language Change* (with Kate Burridge) and the two-volume *Handbook of English Historical Linguistics* (ed. with Laurel Brinton; now available as five-volume paperback) as well as more than fifty papers in high-profile international journals and edited volumes. Alexander Bergs has taught at the Universities of Düsseldorf, Bonn, Santiago de Compostela, Wisconsin-Milwaukee, Catania, Vigo, Thessaloniki, Athens, and Dalian and has organized numerous international workshops and conferences.

About the series

Construction Grammar is the leading cognitive theory of syntax. The present Elements series will survey its theoretical building blocks, show how Construction Grammar can capture various linguistic phenomena across a wide range of typologically different languages, and identify emerging frontier topics from a theoretical, empirical and applied perspective.

Cambridge Elements ☰

Construction Grammar

Elements in the series

The Constructicon: Taxonomies and Networks
Holger Diessel

Constructionist Approaches: Past, Present, Future
Tobias Ungerer and Stefan Hartmann

A full series listing is available at: www.cambridge.org/EICG

Printed in the United States
by Baker & Taylor Publisher Services